From the library of
Betty Russell · Xmas 1995
From Peter to his Mum

D1080407

Tales of the
OLD GARDENERS

Tales of the
OLD GARDENERS

JEAN STONE &
LOUISE BRODIE

d&c
David & Charles

FOR OUR MOTHERS

Rosina Stone and Susan James

A DAVID & CHARLES BOOK

Illustrations by Avis Murray

First published 1994
Reprinted 1995

A catalogue record for this book is available from the British Library.

ISBN 0 7153 0253 1

Typeset in Sabon by ABM Typographics Ltd, Hull
and printed in Great Britain by Butler & Tanner Ltd
for David & Charles
Brunel House Newton Abbot Devon

CONTENTS

A postcard dating from the early years of this century

INTRODUCTION

Gardening, in its many aspects, is a perennially popular subject, but little has been recorded about that special breed of men and women who have spent their lives physically building and nurturing gardens. One hears about those designers and architects who conceived the idea of the landscape park and even those who designed smaller gardens, but what of those men and women who have devoted their lives to constructing, cultivating and tending the plants, when gardening was once labour intensive with little machinery to assist in the hard manual tasks?

Gardeners are often gifted and hold a great bank of knowledge, sometimes passed down from father to son, but frequently learned through practice as they move up the hierarchy of the gardening profession from garden boy to head gardener. By the time they have reached the top, not only have they learned to deal with plants, but also with people, for they are always at someone's service. It might be the owner of a country house, or even the general public if the garden is opened to visitors. It could be a municipal or royal park, a school or factory garden. Furthermore, many gardeners had a large team of men whom they had to manage.

Many country house gardens have now vanished, or passed into the ownership of organisations such as the National Trust or English Heritage. Other owners are well aware of the need to run the gardens and estates along commercial lines with the help of a limited number of staff and more equipment. Technological progress has lightened the gardener's physical load, and fewer hands are needed.

The gardener that remained on the same estate for the whole of his career is an exception, as usually he was obliged to move around to get promotion. Most of them held a certain respect for their employers in spite of the fact that they usually earned a minimum wage, that perks were variable and they were given little free time. However, gardeners are conscientious folk and often work all hours in all weathers if they feel it is in the

The Gardeners' Chronicle *was founded in 1841*

best interest of their gardens. On the whole, they remained loyal to their employers even if these were hard taskmasters, for there were but few tyrants!

The following pages comprise a portfolio of gardeners who have devoted their lives to their profession, whether on the estate of a country house, as nurserymen, or working in public parks. Historical information has been recorded, mostly from retired gardeners. Some amongst surely the most elderly in the country have disclosed their earliest memories of gardening, from when they first started out, sometimes as children, to their experiences in more recent times. They have told of their achievements and disasters, of good times and bad times, relationships, working practices and, frequently, their secrets. All have followed the same profession, but all have a different tale to tell.

Gardeners from all over the British Isles have been interviewed about their work in a variety of gardens, but it is sad that only one lady agreed to be interviewed, although many were contacted. Perhaps in contrast to the men who were on the whole extrovert, lady gardeners of earlier generations were of a shy nature.

We hope you will add the names of all the gardeners that appear in the following pages to the list of garden owners, designers and architects who have previously been honoured for their work.

JEAN STONE
LOUISE BRODIE

NEVER LOOK
BACK
Edgar Spillett
St John's Jerusalem Garden,
Kent

Unlike most gardeners who move around from one job to another to further their career, Edgar Spillett spent more than forty years working in the same garden and for most of these years for the same family. His old-world courtesy and gentle humour must have been well suited to his life as head gardener at St John's Jerusalem, Sutton-at-Hone, Kent: his kind and caring nature earned him not only the love and loyalty of the owners, Sir Stephen and Lady Tallents, but also the affection of their grandchildren who have maintained a lasting friendship with him.

Now in his mid-eighties, Edgar's contented attitude to life has remained with him in his retirement: 'Never look back,' he says, bright blue eyes smiling, 'you make up your mind and look forwards.' Edgar now spends his winters following new crafts – for example, his nimble fingers patiently put together precision models constructed with matchsticks.

Edgar went to work at St John's Jerusalem when he was nineteen, and became head gardener by the time he was twenty-one. Times were hard when he left school in the late twenties and work was not easy to come by, but Edgar found a job in a local garage where he worked mostly as a lorry driver's mate and sometimes drove a taxi. These were the days before driving tests, and by the time he was eighteen Edgar considered he could drive well enough to become a chauffeur. When he was recommended by his firm to become chauffeur at the 'big house', Edgar went down to see the gentleman and was offered the job; and he was very happy to move to the St John's Jerusalem garden where he was taken on at 25s a week, plus his keep.

The house is medieval and once belonged to the Knights Hospitalers of St John whose headquarters were in Jerusalem. Like many monasteries it was disposed of by Henry VIII after the dissolution of the monasteries in 1537, and it became one of England's country houses. The estate passed from one family to another until it eventually became the home of a Mr and Mrs Stephen Tallents (later Sir Stephen, see page 12). The grounds, some forty-five acres, were mainly let out to a farmer, but the gardens comprised some seven or eight acres; about four were cultivated and the rest mown. There is a moat fed by the River Darenth, but unfortunately for one reason and another this now has a tendency to dry out.

Edgar Spillett now lives at Red Oaks, a retirement home in Sussex belonging to The Gardeners' Royal Benevolent Society

Edgar was soon helping in the garden, even though his father, who enjoyed gardening (in spite of the poor financial reward), had advised him: 'Anything except gardening, you're not going into gardening. There's no money in it!' Edgar's mother and father were the local florists, 'doing wreaths and wedding flowers'. His father had trained at Mounts in Canterbury; he had started there at 1s 6d a week, a glass of beer and some bread and cheese at lunchtime – but since he did not drink, it was a poor deal for him! He became a nursery gardener, the owner of a smallholding with three greenhouses. Since as long as Edgar 'had been able to run about', he had from choice helped with his father's garden. As often happens in small family businesses, when he grew up he frequently lent a hand, working evenings and weekends, sometimes even 'digging stuff up by lamplight' after working at the garage all day. It was not unusual for him to be up all night doing floral work, making wreaths and so forth, and still go off lorry-driving in the morning. It was hard, but from these early beginnings his love of plants was nurtured.

When Edgar moved into the 'big house' a new world opened before him. The cook held the most important position below stairs. 'My advice from an old chauffeur at that time was, "Whatever you do, look after the cook, because if you're in with the cook, you'll be in with the lady, and if you're in with the lady it doesn't matter about the old man!" . . . She was a real old Victorian cook and a real terror, but we got on well in the end.'

Later Edgar had a flat outside the estate, but he went in for meals and had to fit in with the strict routine of the house. 'At eleven o'clock it was staff cup of tea, and the gardeners usually came up at that time. The lady came out at half past nine to the kitchen to order the menu, then the head gardener had to come up to see her at ten o'clock to find out what vegetables were wanted. So, when the gardeners brought the vegetables up, they too joined in with a cup of tea.'

Stephen Tallents had a particular interest in fruit and vegetables and in 1934 he was knighted for his work as secretary of the Empire Marketing Board which was responsible for promoting all fruit and vegetable produce from the British Empire. The garden was, therefore, practically all vegetables when Edgar first went to St John's, so as well as potatoes, they grew quite a lot of produce that was not generally available to the ordinary householder at that time: sea-kale, asparagus from the three or four asparagus beds, globe artichokes, and the delicately flavoured salsify, or oyster plant, as it was sometimes known. Chicory was grown under the bench in the greenhouse, but of course outside there was still room for good old-fashioned rhubarb. They also collected sorrel and nettles from the grounds.

Nettles are a versatile plant and useful for many purposes. Once used by the weaver and the dyer, in Scotland it was said that the stalks of old nettles were as good as flax for making cloth; in the thirties it was sought after there for paper making. During the Great War, Germans demonstrated that a range of woven goods, from stockings to tarpaulins, could be produced from the bast fibre which makes up from eight to ten per cent of the nettle stalk. In World War II, truckloads of nettles were exported from Hungary for textile uses in Germany. Nettles are also known for their culinary attributes, and it is said that good 'nettle beer' and 'bubble and squeak' can

be made from the humble nettle. As far back as 1661, Samuel Pepys praised 'nettle porrige'; but the favourite at St John's was nettle soup.

Sir Stephen was also very fond of mushrooms. He knew the precise location of every variety and had a map made showing their exact whereabouts on the estate.

The gardeners were able to keep the house well supplied with vegetables, although they might have to buy a hundredweight of potatoes to get them through the cold weather; cook used to say that all she ever had to buy was 'the occasional tin of peas in winter – everything else was out of the garden'.

When Edgar started work in the garden of St John's he already had a good knowledge of gardening, so there was little to be learned from the head gardener. There were also two young chaps, friends of Edgar whom he had recommended, and a very old gentleman who came down to do a bit of scything. Then the war brought problems as a result of conscription, and after the war the staff was whittled down further, as it was at most country houses. Many estates found they could manage with fewer staff (particularly as machinery was getting more and more proficient), and others could not afford the wages. Eventually by the seventies Edgar was left with only one assistant.

Nevertheless, he always kept the garden in good order. Vegetables eventually gave way to flowers, but Edgar is firm about wild gardens, maintaining that 'A garden is a garden'. He believes there is enough space for insects and so on in the surrounding countryside – though he was still thoughtful in keeping one wall clad with cotoneaster as food for the birds . . . 'who used to leave it till just after Christmas, then they would clear it of berries in a fortnight' he remembers.

Edgar admires naturalness. Among the roots of the copper beech standing majestically before the house he planted hundreds of crocuses as a herald of spring. Multitudes of daffodils were planted randomly throughout the orchard: 'That's the way they should be grown, just naturally, in the grass.' And they grew this way, increasing in number every spring for nearly forty years; but sadly, Edgar recalls that after his retirement the daffodils were mown down at the wrong time and are now lost.

Edgar's gardens were well planned and well planted to give interest all year round. 'Our boast was that we could always find a bunch of flowers in the winter time as well as any other time of the year.' Not only were flowers grown outdoors, the chrysanthemums that Edgar grew in one of the two greenhouses were a speciality.

There were always enough at Christmas time for the church and friends in the village, as well as to decorate the house and give to guests to take home. Tucked away in the corner of one of the greenhouses Edgar kept an orange tree, and many a village lass enjoyed having a sprig of blossom on her wedding day.

There were, of course, tasks that Edgar did not like. He found cutting the lawns tedious work, but there was no escape from this; and cutting hedges he also found to be a complete waste of time. However, later in his life at St John's he was given the opportunity to purchase some mechanical clippers. He went off to the local ironmonger's where they 'got all their stuff from' and when he was asked if he wanted 'electric or battery?' he explained it would have to be battery because the gardens reached some distance from the electricity supply. 'How long does a battery last?' asked Edgar. 'Ooh, about three-quarters of an hour.' Edgar was dismayed. 'What? That's no good to us! It takes two of us all day, along with the other routine jobs as well.' However, the shopkeeper suggested they should take some on

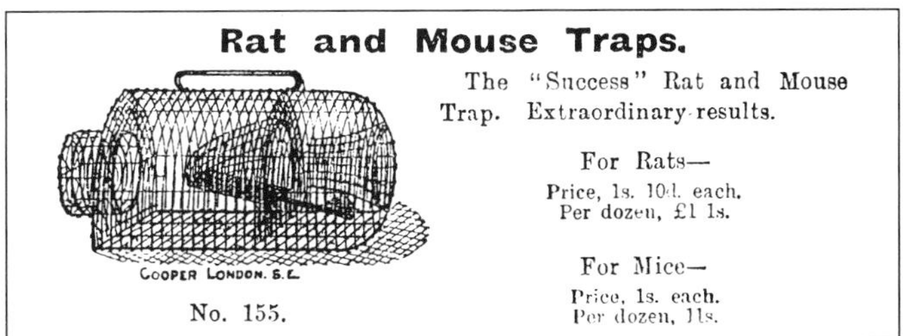

approval, and to their delight they found they could complete about three-quarters of the cutting with one battery, and with practice they were able to get round the complete garden in one go.

A particular attraction of the garden was the collection of willow trees. There were coloured willows, known for the spectacular gold and scarlet of their winter bark; and the white willow, grown at St John's commercially. Many a Kentish cricketer became the owner of a cricket bat made from the white willow of St John's.

Sir Stephen got some willow stock from Long Ashton Research Station and later some from Kew. The stock was further improved by a gentleman who worked at Long Ashton who used to go round and inspect the cricket bat trees after felling and pick out the whitest found that particular year; a truckload of prunings of that tree, suitable for propagation, would be delivered to the railway station and that made up most of the stock.

The willows were planted at twenty-five foot intervals and the average age of the tree when it was felled was about twelve years. The youngest one ready for felling was acknowledged to be ten years old; St John's record was eleven years from the time it was put in. If it took longer than fifteen years for a willow to grow to the correct size, the wood became too hard and heavy. The trunk had to be kept clear of any branches up to a height of seven foot six inches, or approximately up to where a man could just reach, otherwise a knot or stain could deface the matured timber; if even a little branch was left on, a speck would show right through to the centre of the tree after it was felled. The circumference of the tree when ready to be felled was three to four foot – if a man could put his arms round the trunk and his fingers just about met, it was about the size for felling. To leave the willows longer would spoil them. Edgar remembers:

'The outside of the tree is the face of the bat and the cleft is back to the centre. It would be difficult to get the correct cut if the tree was not the right size, so it was better to tell them when it was just about ready. I could look at a tree at that time and tell whether it was a good tree, or whether it was a bad one because you could see what we used to call butterfly marks in it.

'The butterfly marks were a kind of brown patch right the way through the wood as you cut it, and you could see evidence of it on the outside of the bark – if you saw a mark running round the bark you knew there was a butterfly mark there, and that spoilt the tree because the wood must be absolutely pure white. It was never found out exactly why the marks appeared. They used to come and look at the trees and give you a price for them.

'I got quite expert in the end because I knew what they were looking for, so we used to fell about fifty or sixty every three years, when we got going with them. All ours went to Gray Nicolls of Robertsbridge, the famous bat makers. We had Surridges down from Essex, but they didn't offer such a good price. An ordinary tree it was reckoned would produce about thirty-three bats.

'The trunks were sawn into lengths that, once seasoned, would give bat blades of twenty to twenty-three inches. They were then marked and split into clefts that would one day, after seasoning, be formed by a master craftsman into a perfectly balanced cricket bat.'

Sir Stephen Tallents had decided to go into this very specialised project because the property was by the river and willows were the tree natural to the habitat and known to have grown there since the mid-fourteenth century. All sorts of willow were grown experimentally. From the Somerset willow *Salix ramulis aureus* Edgar made little shopping baskets as Christmas presents for the young daughters of the local firemen. Just before Christmas he always cut the *S. daphnoides purpurea*, or pussy willow; shoots were kept in water in a warm place, and with his fingers he would remove the caps from the buds to produce pussy willows for a Christmas flower arrangement.

St John's has a long history that dates back to Roman times, and a corner of the watercress beds is believed to have been a graveyard for Roman horses. Under some cottages south of the Darenth, eleven skeletons were found, feet to the East, and stories of ghosts around the estate have lingered. At night, Edgar's wife and the housemaid used to lean out of the window to chat, with the lights out so that cook would not hear them; and sometimes they would see a grey form looming in the garden, marked by a small light moving before it. They discovered that the form would disappear if they turned on the lights in the house, but if they put the lights out and waited, they would see it again. The tale was told to Edgar – and he chuckled mischievously. He knew all about this: it was Edgar himself. He had been setting snares to catch rabbits and had done it secretly, after dark by torchlight, so that the ladies would not be upset. If the house lights came on, he would stop and wait for a while and then start again after the lights were put out!

Sir Stephen Tallents died in 1958 and his wife in 1968. It was a very sad time for Edgar, even when young Mr Tim Tallents offered to build him a bungalow at Banbury for his retirement. However, Edgar decided to stay on at St John's and must have felt some relief knowing the property had been given to the National Trust. Sadly, there had been no endowment so the house and garden were let to tenants. Mr and Mrs Tom Salter of Gear and Carnaby Street fame were the first tenants to move in, and stayed for three years. They did not interfere with the garden and left it for Edgar to look after. They paid him well, too: 'It was the first time I had got paid well.' That is not to say he held a grudge against the Tallents. 'Times were different then.

'Sir Stephen was a real gentleman, but when the men were working till one o'clock on a Saturday, it was a job to get permission to let them off at noon to go to the football match – and when they tried to get Saturday morning off, it was like asking for gold. You never asked for a raise in salary and never thought about it in terms of trade unions.'

But Edgar will not hear a word against the Tallents: 'You were part of the family.' He recalls that he and his wife were given their wedding and reception by the Tallents at St John's. 'Times were different then, Sir Stephen was a gentleman.'

Various tenants have lived in the property since it has been under the care of the National Trust, but Edgar is still loyal to the Tallents family and his memories of the garden. He retired in 1976, but still went along to help part-time. He said he would retire completely if he saw the place going down, and he did. 'In five years it was a wilderness, in ten, gone completely . . . but never look back,' he smiles, 'you make up your mind and you look forwards!'

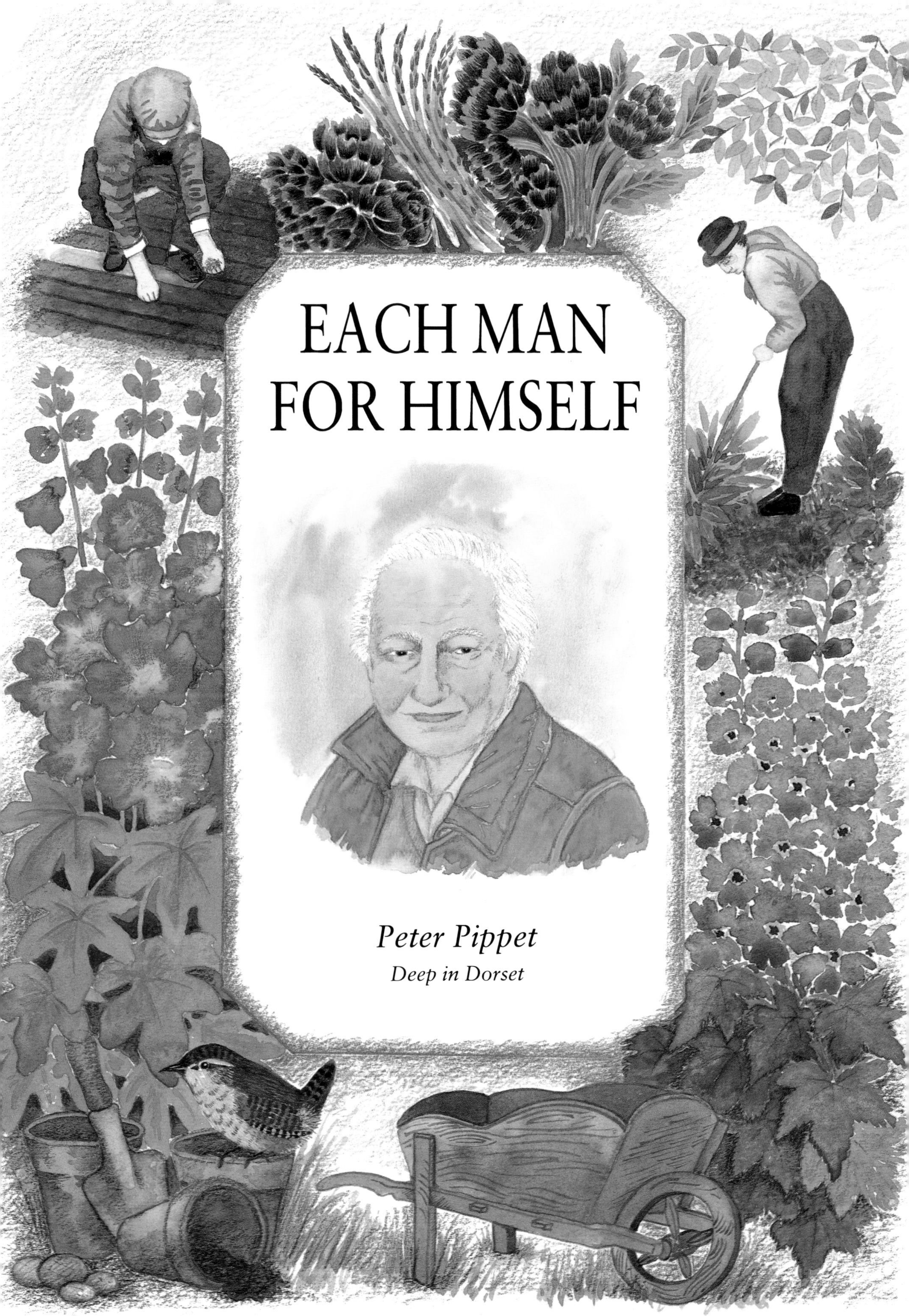
EACH MAN
FOR HIMSELF
Peter Pippet
Deep in Dorset

'Do you know flowers from weeds?' was the question at Peter Pippet's interview. As he says: 'I had to call at the back door, as it were, and then I had to follow the butler through the castle, and the butler had a limp. And I had seen a film with some comedians when the butler had done the same thing, and they would all limp after him! By the time we got through the castle I wasn't at all nervous. Well, I wasn't nervous in any case, 'cos I didn't care if I got the job or not. I didn't know the difference between flowers and weeds, 'cos I didn't have the foggiest idea about gardening, but I said yes, and got the job – I was the only applicant, I guess!'

So in the 1950s Peter moved in to the back lodge, which was a castellated affair, with bars on the windows and door. Peter learned that some years previously the inmates used to be threatened regularly by unsavoury characters demanding food and money, although he never had that problem himself. The lodge had a spiral stone staircase and when Peter asked where to sign on for his ration of coal for heating and cooking, the gardener joked that he would only need a half-hundredweight sack: 'When you get cold, you can just put it on your back and go up and down stairs a few times, you'll be warm enough!'

Peter Pippet is a man who tells a racy story, and his talk is full of the incidents which have happened to him in a life of mixed fortunes. His job perfectly illustrates some of the problems which might have occurred in the life of a gardener working for an unsympathetic employer. The whole village and the farms around belonged to the estate, and many of the cottages were in very bad repair. Old Dick, aged eighty-four, was crippled with rheumatics and so was his wife. There was no stair-rail, and they wouldn't give him one. Then he complained that the roof was leaking, which it was, and they wouldn't do anything about that, either. There was another cottage empty half a mile from the village: 'You can move up there,' they said.

'No I can't, my wife would never be able to get down to the village.'

'Oh well, you won't accept the offer, stay where you are.'

Many of the employees on the estate were elderly. Pay was bad and conditions worse, and there was nothing that the men could do about it. At this date, an owner had the power to make life very uncomfortable for his or her workers. On the other hand, even if wages were low, the people on a good estate would be

Peter Pippet: early days

looked after as part of an extended family, with all the concern and security that this implies. If, however, the owner did not choose to do this, for whatever reason, then the employees could find themselves in a very bad situation, where their housing was substandard, wages were withheld in times of sickness, and with no provision for old age. They were completely powerless.

'I got the flu, and Dick got the flu, and he was off for about four days and I was off for about a week. They stopped his money, not mine. They stopped his because they knew that he couldn't do anything about it. The whole place was run on medieval lines.'

It was difficult for an employee to leave the estate against the wishes of the owner, when it was he who had to supply references. The maintenance man on this estate was promised a job as foreman on a building site in the local town, but when they wrote to his employer for references, he never heard of the job again. In another case, Peter Pippet's friend wanted to move away.

'I shan't give you a reference you know,' he was told.

'That don't matter, I'll write one myself, same as I did when I come here,' came back the smart reply.

'You had to move,' says Peter, 'in order to get a rise and better accommodation.

Otherwise you'd stay at the same rate the whole time.' When Peter himself got another job, the owner again said that he wouldn't give a reference.

'I don't need a reference.'

'It can't be much of a job then,' came the answer.

The big house was surrounded by acres of lawn, lakes and woods, which it was Peter's job to tend. He had never had a thorough training in gardening. His favourite tasks included anything to do with machinery, mending pumps, cutting difficult undergrowth and so on. He could turn his hand to anything. One of his first jobs was hooking (cutting) grass with Dick.

'I didn't realise till I was older quite how marvellous he was for his age. He was bent double but he would hook away, and he taught me how to sharpen the hook, and I became quite a good hooker. I was given a brand new hook, and after the summer I had worn it down, nearly worn it out, 'cos you have to keep sharpening it. There was some grass called devil's grass, a very fine grass, and it didn't half take

some cutting. I got on with Dick on the cross-cut saw too, and just about drove him mad at the start because I was pushing, not pulling, you know.'

The log store gradually filled up – but at the back, the villagers made a hole in the shed and pinched the best wood, leaving the knotted and spitting logs for the fires in the big house. Prunings and odd pieces were placed in the farmyard for burning, as the woodash was needed for potting in the greenhouses (where Peter didn't work). On one occasion the tractor driver set the pile alight with paraffin and the woodash could not then be used for the potting.

The lawns of the house sloped steeply from the terrace, and cutting them could be a dangerous business. Really they should have had two men to do them, and a rope for each mower, but that wasn't always the case. There was so much grass that a small lorry was needed to pick up the cuttings after they had finished.

In the woods an Allenscythe, a large machine on wheels, was used to cut the rough grass, brambles, thistles and nettles. One year Peter, instead of levelling just the walks

through the woods, cut back a much larger area of undergrowth. By January it was covered with snowdrops, which had never been seen before because of the brambles. Later there were also copious primroses, bluebells and cherry trees. As for the lakes, they were becoming choked with reeds which had to be cut back, and they used a punt for this purpose.

There were a few flowerbeds and some rosebeds round the house. Peter helped to dig the kitchen garden, which was two acres in extent. The orchard was large and the fruit, when picked, went into store. The owner's Christmas present to the men was a paltry 2lb of apples! By spring, the surplus had gone rotten, and barrowloads had to be wheeled out to the dump.

When Peter moved in to the lodge on the estate he had no furniture at all, and none was provided. He bought an army surplus bed and had it transported to his new home for ten shillings. He would eat his meals sitting on a step of the staircase, with an old box for a table. One evening there was a knock at the door, which was a most unusual occurrence. 'I'm from the Prudential, perhaps you'd like to insure your furniture?'! Eventually the lady of the house gave him some curtains, as she said that the lodge looked unoccupied. Without rails or any means of hanging them, Peter just nailed them up at the sides of the windows.

The water supply came from a spring to the lodge, but soon it didn't work at all. After a while, Peter got tired of carrying water for all his needs. He went on strike, but then had to spend a good deal of time and effort digging up the pipes to discover the leak and repair the damage. He was earning less than an agricultural wage at the time.

There was no toilet. Peter was expected to use an ancient Elsan in a derelict shelter. He preferred the woods, even with the stinging nettles! When he got married, he bought a new Elsan, which he put into the basement of the lodge with partitions round it.

He told his employer that he was thinking of getting married.

'Do you think that is wise, Pippet?'

'How do you mean, wise?'

'Well, financially.'

'I thought you might give me a rise.'

'Well, it couldn't be much – perhaps 2s 6d a week.'

Next day: 'I don't think we'll give you a rise, Pippet, we'll give you a pint of milk a day.' They had six cows for themselves, they were swimming in milk.

'But that doesn't come to half-a-crown.'

'Doesn't it? I never have to buy milk.'

In spite of this, Peter went ahead and married the nurse he had met at a social club in the New Forest. He had to work on Good Friday, then he travelled all the way to Huntingdonshire where his bride was living at the time, and he had to be back for work as usual after the weekend.

One day, Peter was there when the lady of the house was reading the paper. 'Do you know,' she said, 'that they have put income tax up to 19s 6d in the pound?'

'Then it wouldn't cost you much to put my wages up by a pound, would it?!'

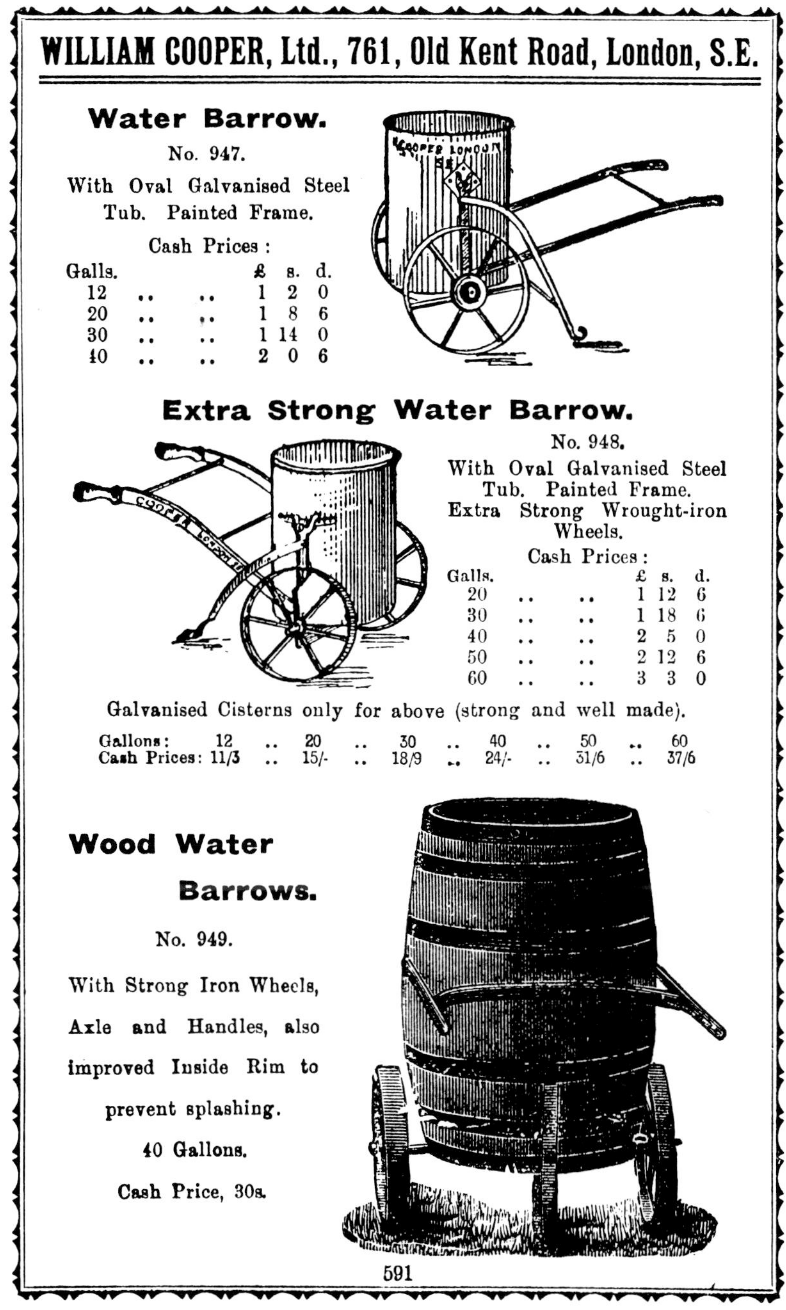

WILLIAM COOPER, Ltd., 761, Old Kent Road, London, S.E.

Water Barrow.

No. 947.

With Oval Galvanised Steel Tub. Painted Frame.

Cash Prices :

Galls.	£	s.	d.
12	1	2	0
20	1	8	6
30	1	14	0
40	2	0	6

Extra Strong Water Barrow.

No. 948.

With Oval Galvanised Steel Tub. Painted Frame. Extra Strong Wrought-iron Wheels.

Cash Prices :

Galls.	£	s.	d.
20	1	12	6
30	1	18	6
40	2	5	0
50	2	12	6
60	3	3	0

Galvanised Cisterns only for above (strong and well made).

Gallons:	12	20	30	40	50	60
Cash Prices:	11/3	15/-	18/9	24/-	31/6	37/6

Wood Water Barrows.

No. 949.

With Strong Iron Wheels, Axle and Handles, also improved Inside Rim to prevent splashing.

40 Gallons.

Cash Price, 30s.

591

replied Peter. Of course that didn't happen, and on his wages he was always short of food; he liked to try and supplement his diet with rabbits, but although he bought snares and set them, he was never able to succeed like his friend the poacher. A throw with a heavy stick might kill a rabbit from time to time, as it tried to escape the approach of the machine demolishing its hiding place.

One day Peter came home to find a bloody head on his kitchen table: the butcher was doing him a good turn, giving him a pig's head. This was before he was married, when he relied for his culinary education on the Ministry of Agriculture wartime

publications. A short read was enough to convince him – the head was buried down the garden.

The lead on the roof of the big house was at that time very valuable. When the nails holding the slates became loose and fell out, it was the custom to use some lead bent round to hold the slate in place and to prevent the rainwater soaking down. In addition, there were sheets of lead covering a flat part of the roof. A fellow employee of Peter's had a regular deal with a scrap merchant:

'He snipped the lead off from round the slates where they met the parapet wall, leaving only an inch or so, instead of the six it should have been. Of course it began to leak. They had a builder in to look at the ceiling in the breakfast room. "I can't afford to have it redone now, I'll wait till it falls down," said Madam. Which it did when she was having breakfast one morning. Apparently she never batted an eyelid. So it was decided to have it reroofed, and a builder was found who would do it for the sake of the lead. The foreman put loads of it in his van to take it away – and this worried my mate, old Tom, because he saw his income disappearing. He persuaded the foreman to split the spoils, and the van was diverted to Tom's cottage. He had so much lead that his bedroom floor nearly collapsed under the weight! He bought a motorbike from the proceeds.'

Peter's experiences can be compared to those of Edgar Spillet who, in complete contrast, was treated by his employers as one of their extended family. Peter remembers this period in his life with wry humour, a characteristic which must have helped greatly to get him through difficult times.

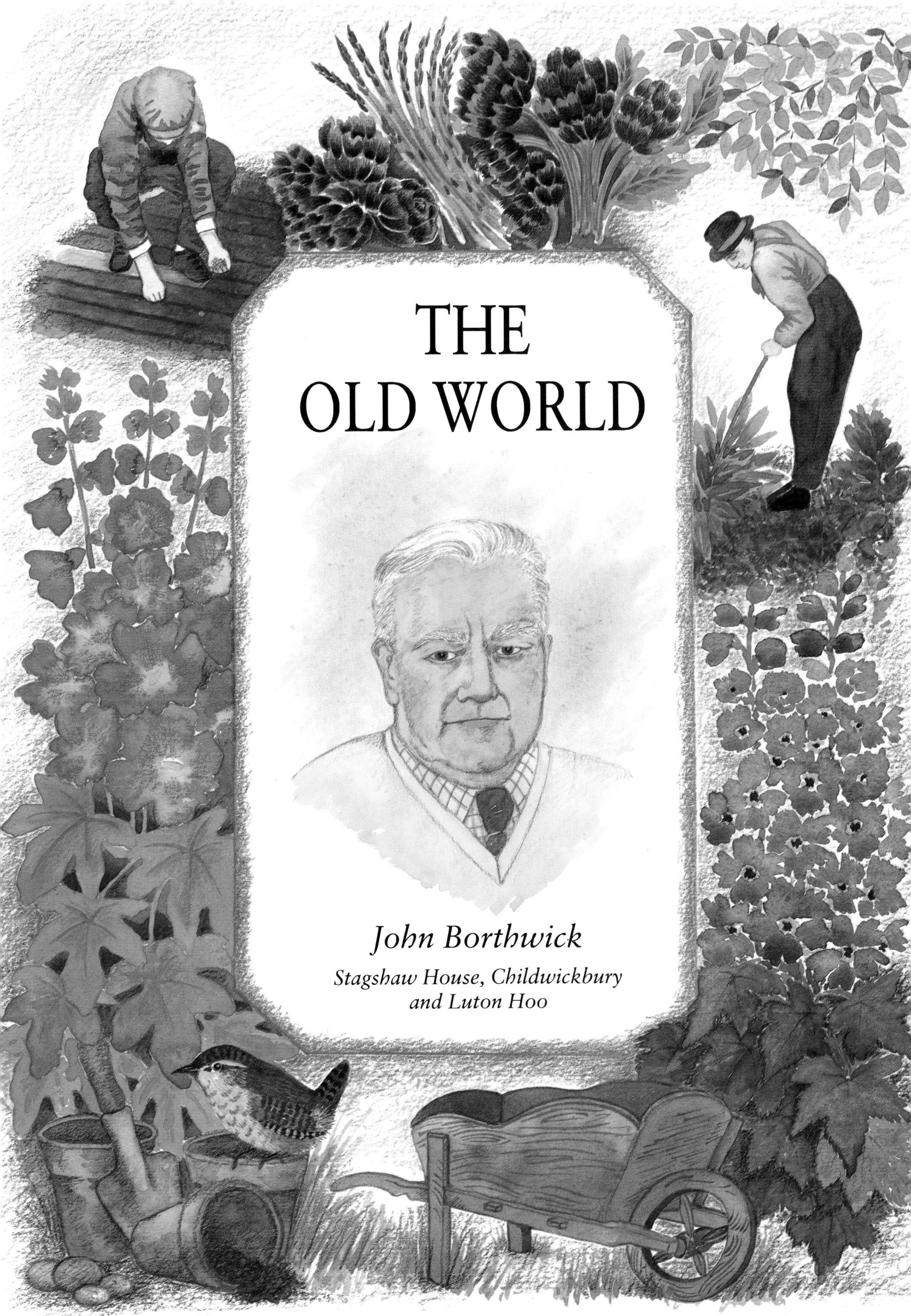
THE
OLD WORLD
John Borthwick
Stagshaw House, Childwickbury
and Luton Hoo

It was the Depression, the late 1920s, when John Borthwick was a boy at school. He felt himself very lucky to earn something, doing odd jobs before and after school at the great house near where he lived. He fed the ferrets, scrubbed the steps and cleaned the shoes. 'Things were very hard, cold winters then, and no work. I was proud to be working at the Hall. The village life in Yorkshire was quite interesting. The Christian ethic was marvellous – everyone was part of the community. It revolved round the mansion and the church.'

On leaving school at fourteen, John worked full time in the gardens at Patrick Bronton Hall. The head gardener trained him well, being very strict but fair, and his warning has remained imprinted on John's memory ever since: 'If you don't put more into gardening than you ever take out, then get out of it now. There's nothing in it for you.'

After four years here, the head gardener suggested he move on, and found him a place in Northumberland. It was common at this time for career moves to be made in such a way, probably the only way they could be made. The head gardeners had the information about job vacancies, and of course controlled the references which were given. There was not a lot of choice. Job security made up for low pay, and the young men stayed where they were till they had learnt everything which that particular place had to offer.

It was a new way of life at Stagshaw House in Northumberland, and John was

John Borthwick as a boy

John outside the greenhouses at Stagshaw in the 1930s

terribly homesick at first. He lived in the bothy, the estate house where all the unmarried boys stayed together. It was the usual practice in the 1930s for each estate to provide communal accommodation for labourers who did not have families living nearby, until they themselves got married and set up homes of their own. The bothy might be a substantial and spacious house, or lodgings with poor facilities, such as an outside toilet and tap; it all depended on the estate's owner.

They had to pay their own way in the bothy at Stagshaw. They had fruit and vegetables and milk from the estate, and meat was bought by the inside foreman who budgeted for them – and 'Woe betide him if it was over 10s a week', which was all they could manage out of their wages. A woman came in to look after them, and she cooked breakfast, cleaned, and prepared lunch. At night each man ate what he could afford. Sixteen young men lived in the bothy at this time, and they were strictly supervised by the head gardener. He would wait outside to make sure that they all appeared right on time for work at 7.30am, and at 10pm he would come round again to make sure that they were all at home and behaving themselves.

Pay day was something to remember: 'The inside foreman would go into the village on his bike and bring all the money back in a Gladstone bag. Then he would go into the inner sanctum, the potting shed. He had this sheet on his desk and a piece of blotting paper above your name and blotting paper below, so nobody knew what anyone else was getting. Funny really. He never soiled his hands, he had hands like a debutante.'

Once John had settled down, he found a 'lovely atmosphere' at Stagshaw House. The owner, Mr Straker, was 'in coal, and looked after the whole neighbourhood. He was ninety when he died and still working. He was buried in the churchyard in the gardens; we kept watch over the coffin in the estate church. It was April time and there were about three hundred wreaths laid out. It was wonderful. Yes, he was well loved. The family used to give a lot of hospitality. I get so angry with the Socialists – they forget what a hive of culture these places were. The whole family was wonderful.'

Services were held regularly in St Aidan's Chapel in the grounds, conducted by the chaplain retained for this purpose; he had his own house there. A more secular activity in which the Strakers also took a great interest was in riding and in the local hunt. The stable block at Stagshaw is built with noble proportions and is kept in very good repair today, as horses are still bred there.

Close to the kitchen area of the mansion stands a game larder; it is a lovely circular shape, built of stone in the early nineteenth century, and the game would be hung there before being plucked and cleaned for the table. There is also an icehouse in the grounds which was built at the same period. The first icehouse in England dates from 1660 and was erected in St James's Park, London, and the idea became popular in this country during the following two centuries. Icehouses could be built as a shaft into the side of a convenient hill, or as a separate structure; they would be lined with brick or stone and sometimes the entrance would be packed with straw for extra insulation. Ice would usually be cut from a frozen lake or river nearby, then packed closely for storage, to be used throughout the year. John says that food used to be stored in the one at Stagshaw, as well as ice, during the 1930s. Now it is overgrown with vegetation.

The estate employed sixty to eighty people in the farms and woods before the war. There were seven women-servants in the house, and the third housemaid, Linda, married John. There were opportunities for them to meet when John brought vegetables to the house, and Linda remembers that she and John did their courting in the mushroom house. It was very common for young people to marry within the estate in those days; having got to know one another, they would go along to local events such as village dances.

The head gardener had twenty men under him. He could be savage, but he was straight in his dealings with his men. 'In those days, gardeners were really thought a lot of by the aristocrats. Well, they depended so much on them, didn't they? The gardeners were well looked after, they had security in their jobs. The aristocrats knew about their people and helped them out of love. They visited the cottages. The Straker family built and maintained a hospital in Corbridge, and all the surplus from the gardens went to the hospital.'

Corbridge today is a little town busy with tourists looking at the Roman and medieval remains. Members of the family still live at Stagshaw House, and their name is well known in the town; the Charlotte Straker Hospital is still there, too. John remembers Charlotte Straker well. 'If the lady came into the garden, you hadn't to speak to her first. This particular lady was a very charming lady, but she always used to wear a very pronounced scent, and the gardeners would smell this, you see, and know she was about.'

Departments included the pleasure garden, kitchen garden, and the glasshouses, which were the most important, at least in John's eyes. Here they grew orchids, carnations, pot plants, camellias, peaches, melons and grapes. Outside there was a rose garden, a rock garden and an herbaceous border, as well as changing features for different times of the year. The wealthy used to support the plant-hunting expeditions abroad, and received seeds and plants in return. Accordingly the Strakers had a Chinese border – some of the seeds came to nothing, but a lot of them did, and John found it interesting to tend them.

The gardens at Stagshaw House today are greatly changed, a state of affairs which reflects the lack of labour. They are, however, beautifully kept – by one man with occasional extra help. The terrace, falling away to an area of flowerbeds, lawns and a tennis court has extensive views over the Tyne valley. Some of the glasshouses have been taken down, others are unused, but they do still grow a few peaches and figs, along with tomatoes and some flowers under glass. A recent addition is a small orchid house.

In John Borthwick's day, the younger employees were given a wide range of experience in the various departments of the garden. Obviously the men were kept very busy in spring, summer and autumn, but, as John says, '. . . winters in Northumberland were quite severe, and it was difficult to find work for everyone who was employed on the estate. One important job was to collect all the rubbish from the summer into one vast area; then a tree was felled and taken there too, and finally a fire was lit and it was fed with the rubbish night and morning through the winter months. All the stuff left after the fire was out used to go back to help fertilise the garden.'

Another winter job concerned the vineries: 'In the glasshouses the bark of the vines was scraped to get all the disease off. The blinds were laid on the floor, the glass was washed, the metalwork washed with paraffin, and any paintwork was done. It was terrific, really. This gentleman was very good on grapes. We had these three huge vineries, and it was interesting because you used to get all the stuff from the slaughter-house, blood, bones and hair and anything else that came along, and in the winter we

used to lay this six inches deep in a trench in the borders and cover the whole lot with flagstones to keep it moist. It never dried out. Periodically you would lift the stones and see these white vine roots pulling into the trough. You never fed any more through the year, that was enough to keep them going.'

War was impending, and after discussion with his friends in the bothy, John and seven others decided to join the Territorial Army. The head gardener was horrified when he found out, because by this time John was his 'understudy'. 'John, you've only done this to get two more weeks holiday out of me!' One Friday, John and the head gardener had as usual spent the whole day preparing fruit and flowers for the weekend house party. John popped into the bothy for a cup of tea. On his return he announced 'Well, that's it. I'm leaving you.'

'What?!?'

'War's been declared.'

'But you can't leave me with all this lot!'

The time spent at Stagshaw remains a golden period in John's life, with the benevolent family, the beautiful setting of the Victorian house overlooking the Tyne valley, and above all the thorough training and the development of his love for the art of gardening. The war altered everything.

After the war, and an interlude in which John had several other jobs, he came to work for Jimmy Joel at Childwickbury in 1973. This is interesting because it was here, as head gardener, that John was able to put into practice much of the training that he had learnt in his early years. Here there was no shortage of money, either, and any problem was put right immediately. (Mr Joel left £40 million to charity when he died in 1992.)

Mr Joel was a great gourmet. They grew melons, peaches, grapes and figs for his personal consumption; they also grew a thousand strawberries in pots, the first ones having to be ready for his birthday in March. 'Then he had lovely borders and the glasshouses all round, and the rose garden. The only thing we didn't have at Childwickbury was the kitchen garden – a pity really, but he was flower mad. He was a Victorian, and it was a typical Victorian garden. If he wanted a hundred carnations in a vase, then it was a hundred carnations and nothing else. One day I said that I could never grow enough carnations to suit him in the place that we had, we needed a new greenhouse. He sent me

straight out to buy one, just like that! Within a month it was up, and we had ordered thousands of carnations from Portugal.'

Mr Joel was a very shy man, and difficult to talk to unless you discussed racehorses or diamonds. John had a set time to see him, which was at 9.30am every Sunday morning. They planned the work for the following week and John received orders for flower arrangements and fruit for all the three establishments which Mr Joel owned, that is, the London flat and the Newmarket property as well as Childwickbury. Gifts from the gardens were sent regularly to the royal family.

Of Mr Joel, John says, 'All these people have fads. His was that he had to have flowers in scarlet which, with black, were his racing colours. I had to produce salvias by the thousand, red carnations and geraniums, and red tulips in the winter.'

Fruit-growing was on an equally lavish scale. Mr Joel liked a melon a day and it had to be perfect. The seed came originally from Lord Carnarvon and John maintains that he has never tasted anything to beat them. 'You have to reckon a hundred days from sowing the seed to eating them. You sow it on six inches of year-old rotted turf with a little mound of compost where the seed is. The secret is to get an even growth. When the plants reach the apex of the glass they develop side shoots, which is where the melons start. There comes a time when you have to stop watering which is why you need an even growth. They all have to be hand-pollinated. The melons mature in a net as they are too heavy for the branch to hold. When they are getting ripe, you only need to open the door and you can smell that bouquet in the air. That is just one of the signs. When the octagonal groove in the top of each melon asserts itself, you have to cut the fruit off the plant and let them rest in their nets for about eight days. Then you take them to the fruit room to lie in the dark on cottonwool beds. Then you take one each day to the house for dinner. It has to be twenty-four hours in the fridge before the butler serves it. What a melon!'

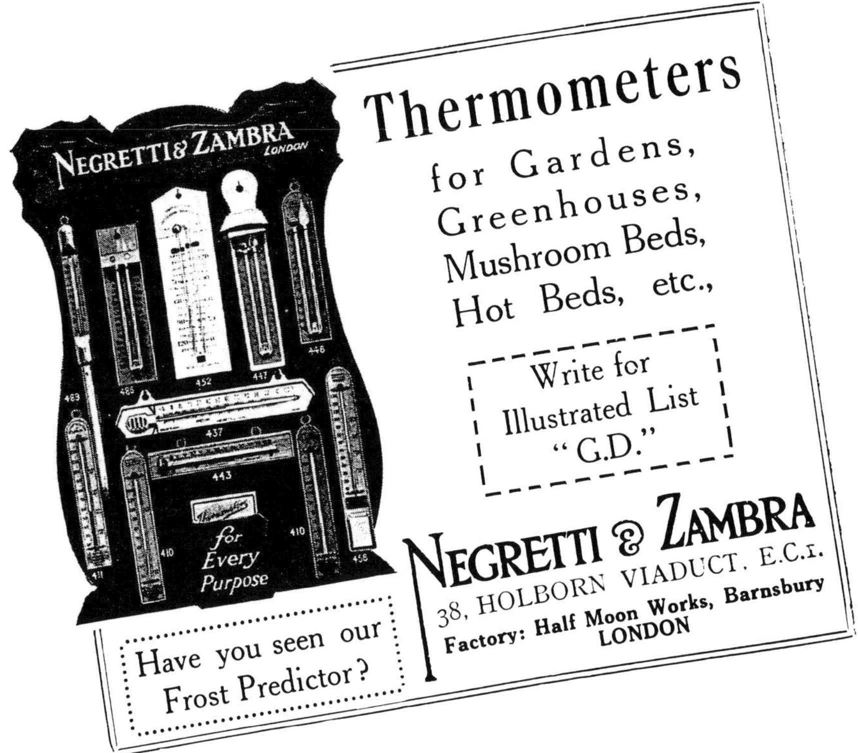

Like the melons, the vines, peaches and nectarines in the greenhouses all had to be pollinated by hand. The middle of the day is the best time for pollination when the flowers are wide open; however, there are not many insects around then so nature was helped along with a rabbit's tail tied to a stick. John also kept bees in the garden to help with the process. One year he brought a hatful of bees into the glasshouse when he thought the time was right, but they wouldn't go near the plants and flew right back to the hive. Ten days later the pilot bees had found their own way to the fruit flowers, and then they all came along to complete the pollination in the natural way.

John's pay was very fair. The accommodation was good and Mr Joel was always generous at Christmas, with a cheque, a turkey, and an outing for the staff to London. There were also cheques at Easter and holiday time. 'It was a wonderful job. I had learnt all this sort of gardening before the war, and not had much of a chance to put it into practice before I came here.' Eventually Childwickbury was sold, which of course meant that John had to change work and home once more.

John came to Luton Hoo in the spring of 1980. He had never seen a garden in such a sorry state in his life, and he really felt that he was too old to tackle the problem. In 1899 the *Journal of Horticulture and Cottage Gardener* gave a description of Luton Hoo. The glasshouses were evidently fantastic, based on those at Sandringham. Eighty thousand bedding plants were used annually in the extensive flower gardens. There were nearly a hundred acres of pleasure grounds near the house, and six acres of kitchen gardens. There was a peach wall a hundred yards long. Grapes, figs and oranges were grown under glass, as well as numerous varieties of flowers such as camellias, cannas, pelargoniums, chrysanthemums and carnations. There was also a rose-house for growing roses under glass.

Today, one can still see the elegance of structure of the Victorian glasshouses. They are, however, disused and overgrown, with loose panes in the roof. The bothy, where the unmarried men were quartered, is still there, facing the head gardener's home where Roy Evans, the present head gardener, now lives, as John did before him. In 1899 the house was considered to be '. . . a good feature of the establishment, conveniently situated near the offices. It is a solid, square-built erection, possessing superior accommodation.' From the outside it still looks solid, as does the bothy, which is unoccupied. Then, it was said that the 'comfort of the young men had been well studied'.

John's friends told him that he was mad to take on the job, but he decided to try – and after a couple of years they were growing strawberries, loganberries, blackberries, blackcurrants, melons and figs, all sorts of fruit. They had to supply the family and their staff. They produced good peaches again too, by feeding them well, pruning severely and tying back. It is important to know when to pick this sort of fruit; peaches and nectarines need sun to give them colour, and the flavour needs time to develop. Supermarket fruit is often picked too early for full flavour, in order to avoid bruising with transport, and to allow time before it deteriorates.

There was no proper kitchen garden at Luton Hoo. John made a herb garden, but observed: 'Then when you have made it, no one knows how to use the herbs!' The rose garden was worn out, and needed a lot of money spending on it, money which was not available. They had a lot of herbaceous beds, as there was not enough labour to provide the extensive bedding plants used before the war; they had tennis courts

Tending chrysanthemums in the early years of this century

and summer houses to care for in the leisure area; and altogether there was a great deal to be done.

The rock garden, at some distance from the house, had a special ambience, but needed care and attention. The following year, in 1981, Roy Evans was employed to do this job. The garden had been created in a hollow, and a massive cliff of craggy York stone had been built as a backdrop; this had been arranged with a grotto at its foot, so that picnics might take place there. A magnificent waterfall was powered by huge pumps, switched on from the house. Rhododendrons, azaleas, daphnes and alpines were planted there. Roy's sole responsibility was to restore this area, just as the other nine gardeners at that time had their own areas of specialisation. Today, as head gardener in his turn, and with only three others to help him, Roy has to do anything that needs doing. What he learnt years ago, comes in useful now. 'Work-wise, everything has to be done the same. You just have to get on and do it yourself.'

Labour costs dictate the plans at Luton Hoo today. Staff numbers are much reduced and this trend is continuing. Mechanised equipment such as hedge shears has taken the place of the hand-operated tools. The owner lives in a separate house now, and Luton Hoo itself is used for conferences. It is also open to the public on a regular basis, but apart from the visitors and the security staff, there are no voices echoing round the mansion. Thus it is cheaper to buy in pot plants for the day they are needed, rather than for the gardeners to grow a constant supply of blooms which may go to waste. It all comes back to labour costs.

When Roy came in 1981, John Borthwick was head gardener. The two men were examples of the old school and the new school of gardening, with different ideas and different ways of doing things. Instead of growing plants on compost, Roy was used to using loam and peat-based ready-mixed preparations; as every bag is the same, you don't need to spend hours sifting through it till it is perfect. Instead of using clay pots, plastic pots were available, being easy to clean when dipped in a weak mixture of Jeyes fluid; new varieties of flowers were coming onto the market.

People who liked working outdoors did not generally like working under glass, and vice versa. John was someone who always preferred to work in the glasshouses. As Roy says: 'When it is bitterly cold outside and your hands are dropping off and your ears are out to here – they are inside in their shirt sleeves, rubbing their hands in glee!'

Up until about 1990, the feeling on the estate was like that of a village: there was the social club, with its bar acting as a focus, and everybody knew everybody; sons and daughters would have married within the estate for generation after generation. Now, Roy says, it is all different, probably because of the redundancies, in the gardens, among the keepers, on the farm and in the builders' yard. Because of this, quite a few of the people have moved away from the estate and there has been an influx of people renting the empty property. They are all outsiders with different lifestyles, and '. . . You don't know them from Adam – or Eve'.

In spite of the variations in their training, and in their gardening careers, both John Borthwick and Roy Evans agree on one thing: loyalty is the key quality in private work – you are doing it for the family.

The Oldest Gardener?

GEORGE Cook was 104 years old in June 1993. The son of a gamekeeper, he was born on the Tilgate House estate, near Crawley in Sussex; eventually he became head gardener there. 'We had one of the best gardens in the south of England, with two acres of walled kitchen gardens. The soil was a poor clay. In the early days we took the topsoil off, got a couple of men with wheelbarrows and a horse and cart, and got some more soil from the fields. Then we dug a trench against the wall in the garden and put concrete in the bottom with the soil on top. Then we planted the fruit trees. After a few years, you find that they are shooting a lot of wood, so you chop the roots off against the concrete. Having the concrete there, you can control the roots and grow more fruit.'

This story is borne out by an article in the *Journal of Horticulture* in 1902: 'Hardy fruit on the open walls are growing and bearing in a manner which shows that skill is brought to bear on their culture. The soil by the walls in which they are planted is all forced – that is, it is specially selected soil brought and put there. Whenever the estate carter is out and about, if his cart is to be empty on the homeward journey, he has orders to seize the opportunity and bring back road-soil or turf parings if the latter are found.'

George remembers his three grape-houses, first crop, second crop and late grapes. The gardeners had to get up at four or five in the morning to thin them out, as this was the best time of day to see them properly against the glass, before the light got too strong. The changes which George saw over the years included new plants, pot plants and plant hybridisation, but he still thought some of the Victorian ways were best. 'You would see me about July or August with a barrowload of 2lb paper bags. I would slip them over the pears all along and tie them up – it looked like a snow storm! But then you didn't have to lay in bed and worry about the wasps and the birds. I put on hundreds. We knew when it was time to pick each variety.'

George aged 104

The Golden Age

WILLIAM has enjoyed his life as a gardener and says that his employers were good to him. Unashamedly, he now talks of one particular frustration: 'There was more satisfaction in a job years ago. It didn't matter how long a job took, so long as it was done properly and to last. With the modern age it is that you clip over it quick, and this is all it is. You are not allowed the time to do a proper job to-day, and that is the day and age. It's frustrating to the older person. To the younger person, I don't think it makes any difference because he's brought up in that way. As I always said, in gardening, if you do a job properly, it lasts. If it's clipped over and quick, you've got to be back to it again in a short time.'

Boiled Nettles

GATHER nettle tops in springtime when still young and tender. Wash thoroughly in cold water, and cook as for spinach with a little water in the bottom of a saucepan for fifteen to twenty minutes, depending on age. Strain through a colander and chop up finely. Serve with a knob of butter. *Alternatively for Nettle purée*, rub through a sieve and mix with butter and cream.

Here We Go

'I thought all dahlia growers placed inverted flowerpots on their stakes to trap earwigs.'
'Correct!' I said. 'It's an old fashioned method, but effective. You fill the pots with dried grass, and the earwigs which infest most dahlias crawl into these for shelter during the daytime, being night prowlers. And what was the second point?'
'Well,' said Robinson, 'is it your opinion that gardeners as well as plants need occasional draughts of some kind of liquid?'
When I nodded assent he couldn't resist the temptation to say
'Then, earwig-o!'

Raymond W.B. Keene *Over the Garden Fence*, 1946

The Garden

. . . How well the skilful gardener drew
Of flowers, and herbs, this dial new,
Where, from above, the milder sun
Does through a fragrant zodiac run,
And, as it works, the industrious bee
Computes its time as well as we!
How could such sweet and wholesome hours
Be reckoned but with herbs and flowers?

Andrew Marvell, 1621–78

London in Spring

'ONE of my great pleasures in London in the early spring is going to the exhibition of the Royal Horticultural Society, at the Drill Hall, Westminster. I think all amateurs who are keen gardeners ought to belong to this society – partly as an encouragement to it, and also because the subscriber of even one guinea a year gets a great many advantages. He can go to these fortnightly exhibitions, as well as to the great show at the Temple Gardens in May, free, before the public is admitted. He has the run of the society's library in Victoria Street; he receives free the yearly publications, which are a series of most interesting lectures; and he is annually presented with a certain number of plants.'

Mrs C.W. Earle, 1896

The Temple Gardens, London

LAWYERS have worked in the Inner and Middle Temples since at least the fourteenth century, and have enjoyed the use of the gardens which run down to the Thames. In 1601 'it was laid out with large and lovely walks . . . ornified with beautiful banks, curious knots and beds of fragrant flowers and sweet herbs of sundry scents'. These formal designs were changed, probably at the end of the eighteenth century, to the more natural landscaped effect that can still be seen today. In the middle of the nineteenth century a final embankment of the river Thames greatly increased the size of the gardens. There is a legend that the two roses used as emblems in the Wars of the Roses were picked from these gardens (Lancaster – *Rosa gallica* var. *officinalis*, and York – *Rosa* x *alba 'Semi plena'*.

Geoffrey Sleeman is head gardener there today. 'Being a gardener is a way of life, a state of mind, not just working at gardening. You've got to build your life around it sometimes, and I really mean that. My wife knows it's true, because there have been many times since we've been here that we've gone out in the car on a Sunday and we've got to the country and I've said "Look, I'm sorry, we're going to have to go home. It's turned sunny and I've got to go and shade and ventilate the greenhouse". She's been furious, but she sees my point of view now. If you think about your gardening in your free time, then I'll give you credit for being a true gardener.

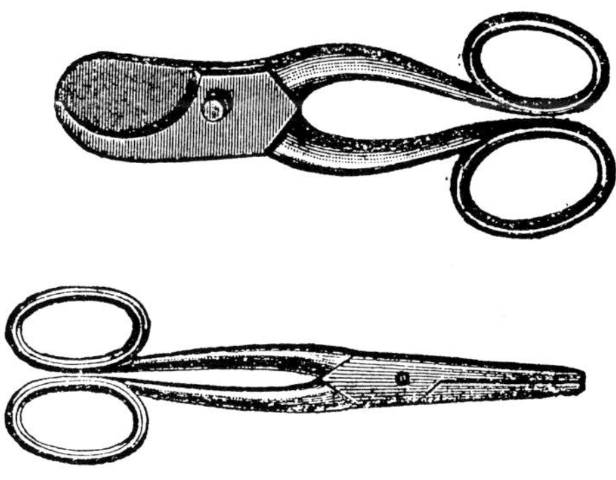

'The Temple is a strange place to work, not everybody likes it here. When people have perhaps been used to working for the councils in parks, it's odd to have young barristers walking round the garden at lunch-time talking in very posh voices. If people are very working class – and I'm not being snobby, I'm just being factual – they don't like it. I've heard a lot of lawyers going round saying "Ha! ha! ha! ha!", and the gardeners assume that they are laughing at them. There's a lot of class distinctions here. And also there's a lot of windows looking over this place and people get the feeling they are being watched all the time. My answer to that is, "Well, as long as you're working, does it matter?"'

CLIPPINGS

Drudgery

IN 1766 a man was employed at the University of Oxford Botanic Garden who was responsible for keeping up the temperature in the hothouses during the night. His chore was to wheel a barrowload of smouldering charcoal up and down the hothouses all night.

The Perils of Plant Collecting

FEW realise the great hardships and dangers which have to be faced in order to secure new plants for cultivation in Europe. In the warmer regions there is a danger from miasma, fever, animals and snakes. Not infrequently too, the collector has to seek his specimens among savage or semi-civilised peoples, who, in most instances, strongly resent his intrusion into their midst; thus seldom a year passes without toll being exacted in one way or another.

George Forrest *Gardeners' Chronicle*, 1910

Tulips

THE gentleman of the house told me, 'If I delighted in flowers, he believed that he could show me such a blow of tulips as was not to be matched in the whole country.'

I was very much pleased and astonished at the glorious show of these gay vegetables, that arose in great profusion on all the banks about us . . .

I accidentally praised a tulip as one of the finest I ever saw; upon which they told me, it was a common Fool's Coat. Upon that I praised another, which it seems was but another kind of Fool's Coat . . . He then showed me what he thought the finest of his tulips, which I found received all their value from their rarity and oddness, and put me in mind of your great fortunes, which are not always your greatest beauties.

Joseph Addison, 1672–1719

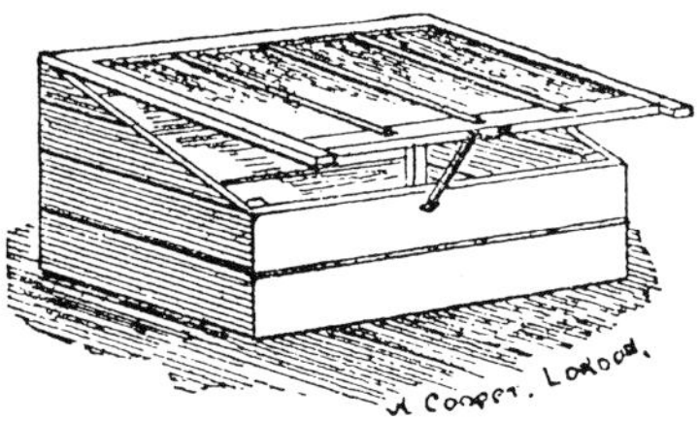

Some Lines on 'Cyclamen'

How shall we sound its mystic name
Of Greek descent and Persian fame?
Shall 'y' be long and 'a' be short,
Or will the 'y' and 'a' retort?
Shall 'y' be lightly rippled o'r,
Or should we emphasise it more?
Alas! The doctors disagree,
For 'y's' a double quantity.
Some people use it now and then,
As if 'twere written 'Sickly-men';
But as it comes from *kuklos* Greek,
Why not 'kick-laymen', so to speak?
The gardener, with his ready wit,
Upon another mode has hit;
He's terse and brief – long names dislikes,
And so he renders it as 'Sykes'.

From an old-time gardening periodical

Blossoms

OF all the propensities of plants, none seem more strange than their different periods of blossoming . . . The vernal crocus expands its flowers by the beginning of March at the furthest and often in very rigorous weather, and cannot be retarded but by some violence offered, while the autumnal, the saffron, defies the influence of the spring and summer, and will not blow till most plants begin to fade and run to seed. The circumstance is one of the wonders of creation, little noticed because a common occurrence, yet ought not to be overlooked on account of its being familiar, since it would be as difficult to be explained as the most stupendous phenomenon of nature.

Gilbert White,
letter to the Hon Daines Barrington, 1778

CLIPPINGS

Aster.

Sayings

The perfect gardener is defined as the person who does the right thing at the right time.

What a man needs in gardening is a cast-iron back with a hinge in it.

One sure way to lose another woman's friendship is to try to improve her flower arrangements.

A weed is no more than a flower in disguise.

The best place to look for a helping hand is at the end of your own arm.

Quoted by Gordon Miller

Sketches and Hints on Landscape Gardening

TO improve the scenery of a country, and to display its native beauties with advantage, is an ART which originated in England, and has therefore been called *English Gardening*; yet as this expression is not sufficiently appropriate, especially since Gardening, in its more confined sense of *Horticulture*, has been likewise brought to the greatest perfection in this country, I have adopted the term *Landscape Gardening*, as most proper, because the art can only be advanced and perfected by the united powers of the *landscape painter* and the *practical gardener*. The former must conceive a plan, which the latter may be able to execute; for though the painter may represent a beautiful landscape on his canvas, and even surpass Nature by the combination of her choicest materials, yet the luxuriant imagination of the *painter* must be subjected to the *gardener's* practical knowledge in planting, digging, and moving earth . . .

Humphry Repton, 1795

Bloomers

They gardened in bloomers, the newspapers said,
So to Kew without waiting all Londoners sped,
From the tops of the buses they had a fine view
Of the ladies in bloomers who gardened at Kew.

Quoted by Gordon Miller

Ground Elder

THE gardens at Pembroke College, Cambridge, are justly famous. During the 1960s the dean of the college was Dr Meredith Ballard Dewey, who was a very knowledgeable gardener and a considerable character. One day the head gardener, Gordon Miller, was given a pot of variegated ground elder, which is much slower-growing than the usual invasive variety. He put it into the cold frame till a suitable home could be found for it. When the dean discovered it, he was horrified. 'Get rid of it, get rid of it,' he said. 'Now we are talking about it,' said Gordon, 'I can understand why it is called "elder" because the leaf shape is very similar to the bush and the flowerhead is similar to the elder flower. I know too that it is called "gout weed" because the Romans are said to have introduced it as a medicinal cure for the disease when you boil the roots; but why is it sometimes called "bishop's weed"?' 'That's easy. In this country we have bishops, and in Scotland they have elders, and neither of them are any damn good!' In fact modern herbalists confirm the efficacy of the plant. The roots and leaves can be boiled together to be drunk as a tea which has kidney flushing properties. It is also recommended as a fomentation to be applied externally to swollen joints.

Rose Aster.

Situations Vacant –
Ornamental Hermits for Landscape Parks

THE Hon. Charles Hamilton of Painshill, Cobham, built a hermitage, upon a mound, in the more gloomy depths of his beautiful grounds. The building had an upper apartment supported in part by contorted legs and roots of trees and although it is said to have been a 'beautiful retreat', Horace Walpole remarked 'it is the sort of ornament whose merit soonest fades, it being almost comic to set aside a quarter of one's garden to be melancholy in. However, it was not Charles Hamilton's intention that he himself should be melancholy, and he offered a seven-year contract for a hermit to be melancholy on his behalf. The agreement made the usual demands. He would, 'be provided with a Bible, optical glasses, a mat for his feet, water for his beverage and food from the house. He must wear a camlet robe, and never, under any circumstances, must he cut his hair, beard, or nails, stray beyond the limits of Mr Hamilton's grounds, or exchange a word with the servant.'

John Timbs *English Eccentrics*, 1866

Lack of conversation or possibly drink was said to have been this hermit's downfall. He was promised 700 guineas if he remained for seven years; however, if 'driven to madness by intolerable tickling of beard, or scratching of robe, broke the condition: not a penny!'

Some sought work as hermits:

A young man, who wishes to retire from the world and live a life of an hermit, in some convenient spot in England, is willing to engage with any nobleman or gentleman who may be desirous of having one. Any letter directed to S. Lawrence (post paid) to be left at Mr OTTON'S, No 6. Coleman's Lane, Plymouth, mentioning what gratuity will be given, and all other particulars, will be duly attended.

The Courier, 11 July 1810

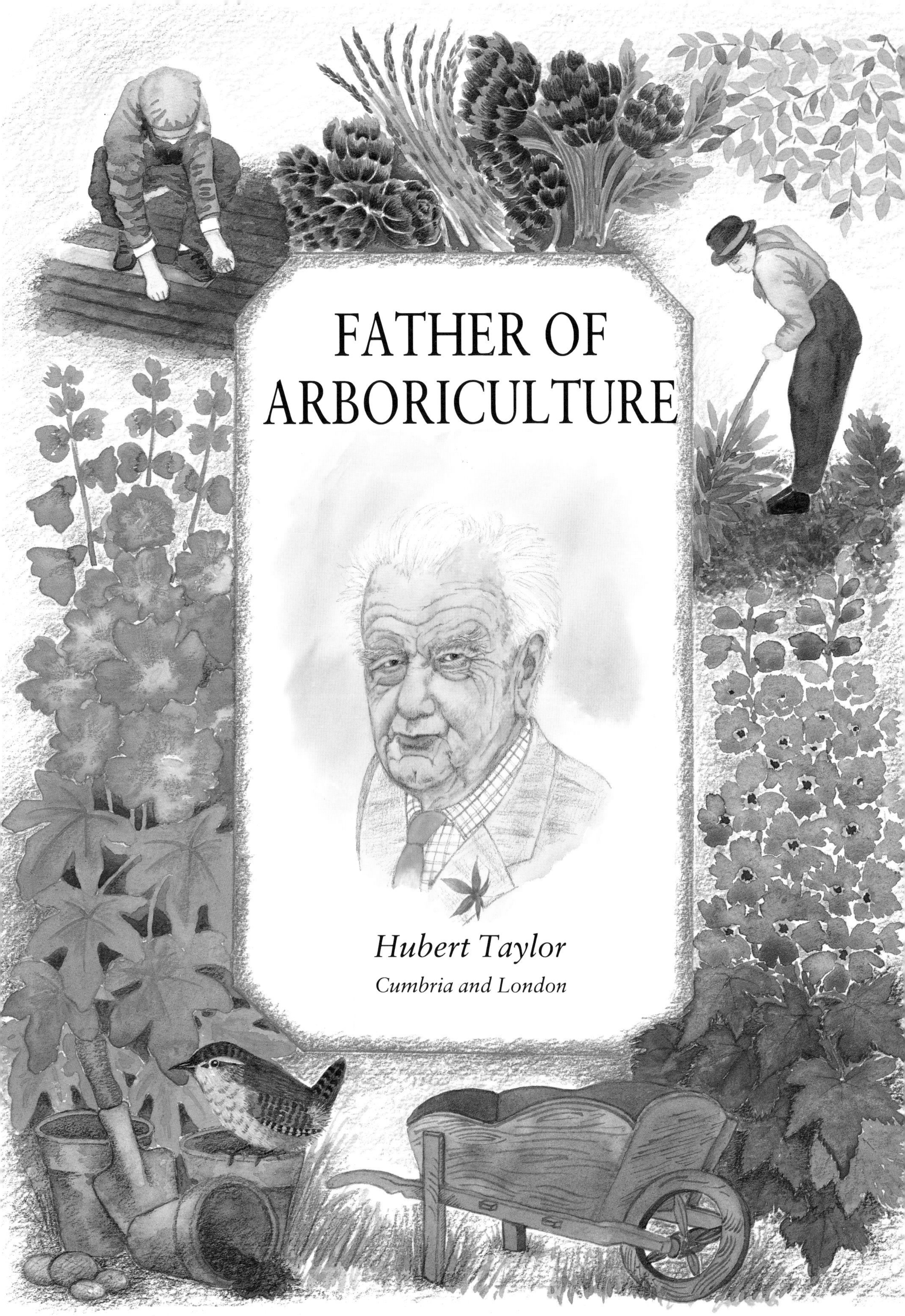
FATHER OF
ARBORICULTURE
Hubert Taylor
Cumbria and London

Hubert Taylor was the son of a Westmorland quarryman and was born in 1908 in the village of Brathay, near Ambleside, in England's Lake District. As a boy he had set his heart on becoming a blacksmith and spent every weekend at the village forge helping with the horses; when he wasn't there, he would be enjoying himself up in the fells where he was often given the task of watching over molten lead used in fence construction.

Encouraged by his father, Hubert's second passion was wild flowers, and he competed in local horticultural competitions even before he started work – this was a way of winning books that he would otherwise have been unable to afford. Perhaps it was this enthusiasm that prompted his parents to put him to work at Hayes and Sons, the local nursery and landscaping firm, where he started just before his fourteenth birthday. Sometimes he enjoyed the work, but weeds grow quickly in the wet climate

of the Lake District and he found the monotony of weeding day after day very tedious. The day began with an early start at seven o'clock, there would be half an hour for breakfast and an hour for lunch. Wages were low at 2s 6d a week, and when the Depression was at its most severe the men were even glad when the firm won a contract to dig trenches for pipes and cables.

Hubert had heard the old tale that boys were sent to garden if they were not much good for anything else, but he was ambitious: 'Right, I'll show them,' he thought, and took it upon himself to go to evening classes to learn shorthand. The gardener was the only one to pass his exams in that first year.

The lad did well at Hayes and Sons, and eventually he was made chargehand. He enjoyed this, particularly as it involved travelling around the north of England on landscape garden work; he was also able to take part in shows held in Glasgow, Shrewsbury and Southport, and in 1926 he was involved in the Royal Horticultural Society Chelsea Flower Show in London.

CHELSEA, 1924.

AWARDED R.H.S. GOLD MEDAL AND "DAILY GRAPHIC" CUP FOR BEST ROCK AND WATER GARDEN.

◈ ◈

Mrs. HAYES RECEIVING THE CUP.

HAYES & SONS,

KESWICK and AMBLESIDE

(ENG. LAKES).

Specialists in Designing Rock and Water Gardens, Heather Gardens and other Landscape Work.

PLANS PREPARED - - ADVICE BY APPOINTMENT
ILLUSTRATED CATALOGUE ON APPLICATION.

Hubert Taylor's first job, started just before his fourteenth bithday, was at Hayes & Sons, Ambleside, Westmorland (now Cumbria)

Hubert stayed with Hayes and Sons until 1929, and then he was awarded a bursary to go to the John Innes Institute at Merton in Surrey, where he particularly enjoyed plant breeding. It must have been this interest which, in 1931, secured him a studentship at the Royal Botanic Gardens, Kew, where he gained a diploma in horticulture. Next he went on to Reading University, to be awarded yet another diploma with distinction, this time in horticultural technology.

For the next five years Hubert held various posts in several county councils, first teaching gardening in schools, then in charge of a fruit and vegetable experimental station, and as Commercial Fruit and Vegetable Advisory Officer. As war developed he had nearly 4,000 horticultural holdings under his wing.

During World War II, Agricultural Food Committees were set up and Hubert did advisory work and lectured on food production. He served in the fire brigade and the Home Guard and advised on camouflaging aerodromes. In 1947 the advisory service was nationalised – at that time it went against the grain for Hubert to work for a nationalised service, so he sought an appointment with the London County Council in the parks department. Hubert became the first Horticultural Advisory Officer to be appointed by the London County Council, and he was made responsible for over 1,800 acres of parkland and woodland in and around London. His major responsibilities were Battersea Park, Victoria Park, Hampstead Heath and Parliament Hill Fields. Only the Royal Parks and City of London areas did not come under his care.

One of Hubert's duties was to supervise the care of sports grounds. There were forty bowling greens, numerous putting greens, three golf courses, football pitches and many grass tennis courts.

Grass is the most important ground cover in parks, it is essential in sports grounds, and pleasing to the eye in leisure areas, and Hubert was conscientious in seeking out

the best turf available. Every year he used to take a trip up to the now Cumbrian coast, and starting north of Blackpool, he travelled as far as the Solway Firth choosing many acres of sea-washed turf on the way. He was careful to see that the turf did not contain weeds, especially plantain and annual meadow grass which were sometimes prolific in flood plain areas. 'I would see it marked out by the acre and later see that it came from the selected area.' He would be given a sample, the deal would be sealed with a handshake, and it would later be purchased by the council's Supplies Department.

Hubert's son, Clive, was keen to follow in his father's footsteps and work outdoors. Early in the 1960s he served an apprenticeship on a golf course as a greenkeeper, and ultimately became an expert on caring for turf.

A large part of every summer's day would be devoted to grass cutting and coping with any disease found in the turf. Fine turf creates a false environment where the spores that cause dollar spot and fairy rings are just two of the diseases that thrive easily. Clive was taught how to spray with the correct chemicals to combat the diseases – one product involved a metallic green powder which, when mixed with water and sprayed onto the turf, transformed it to a beautiful green. Unfortunately, protective gloves were not considered necessary at that time, and for some days after the job was complete those doing the spraying looked as if they were wearing green gloves! Clive remembers that 'Things were haphazard. To-day, jobs are more specialised and it is compulsory for someone spraying to have a certificate of efficiency.'

During the war, changes were made in London's parks. Some had allotments and some open spaces were ploughed up and cereal crops grown, but these changes were temporary. The Marshes at Hackney were, however, changed permanently for the better. The marshland had become a dumping ground for wartime rubble from the

blitz, and later this proved to be an ideal foundation for a series of football pitches which have been used regularly by football teams from schools, boys' clubs and sports' clubs ever since.

A major problem caused by the London blitz was the damage to its trees, and it was a part of Hubert's job to survey blitzed trees and to decide which were to be retained and which taken down. Many were 'blast shaken', and it was necessary to bore into a tree to assess the internal damage; only then could it be decided whether it was safe enough to be left standing. 'They may have looked perfect, but the inner trunk wood had lost structure and become rubbery. Many were pitted with shrapnel – if a chainsaw struck a piece of shrapnel left in a tree it could be very dangerous for a tree surgeon.' Hubert's son, Clive, who has inherited his father's love of trees, tells us that '. . . if ever there is any doubt, trees are now gone over with a metal detector to confirm whether or not there is still shrapnel embedded there.'

Neglect in the war years had caused trees to overlap. They had been planted too close fifty or more years earlier, but if Hubert wanted to remove trees to give others more space, he met with a lot of opposition from members of parliament, as well as the general public. However, eventually they saw sense. 'A tree ought to be saved because it is a living thing, but honestly, if you have got to mutilate others in order to preserve an already mutilated specimen, why not take that one out and let the others be free? Then you save money, because instead of having to prune every second year, if you take one out at one expense, there will be very little expense from then on.'

Realising that trees needed something more than the customary 'short back and sides treatment', Hubert set up the first local authority Arboriculture Department and endeavoured to eliminate the bad treatment and mutilation of trees by way of thorough training of the workforce, particularly in natural pruning. This method encouraged the natural growth and shape of trees. '"Skill, not kill" was my motto, and I had a rubber stamp with the slogan embossed on it, and all our division's tree documents were marked with it.'

The workforce was London's first mechanised tree preservation team. The men did not take too kindly to mechanisation, but they soon came round and saw the folly of using a handsaw when a chainsaw could do the same job more efficiently, using a lot less time and effort.

Hubert introduced elevators for tree work on the streets of London, and stump clearers from the United States of America. The stump clearers had a rotating cutting cylinder that grated away old tree stumps below soil level. 'It was very successful on oak, but unfortunately did not work on poplars whose stumps held water, shredded like cotton wool and clogged the machine. However, within forty-eight hours of receiving a complaint, the designer was over from the US to get things right.'

Digesters, or branch shredders, were also brought into use for the first time and Hubert went over to Paris to make a visit to the firm that made them: 'I had a splendid time over there. With the machines that is!' he added, with a twinkle in his eye. All this mechanisation is commonplace now, but back in the sixties the London County Council was the first to modernise its equipment through mechanisation, and set the pace for other councils around the country.

Clive Taylor had his introduction to arboriculture when he was working on the golf course in the early days of his career, but it was not until the late 1970s that he became seriously involved; and although he learned many of his skills from men in the field, his employers, the Reigate Council, also sent him on courses which taught him how to climb trees, the sectional felling of trees, and about pruning. On one occasion he was taught by a man who had been taught by his father. Clive's training has made him safety conscious, particularly since he had an accident (although it was very minor). His advice is:

'Never go above ten foot without hitching yourself on. It does take longer to get to the top, but it keeps you out of trouble. Try not to use a chainsaw up a tree if you can help it, use a bow-saw. It's harder work, but much safer. It's an art; there's climbing, and there's climbing with a chainsaw – they are two different things completely. A kickback and you are in trouble; there's only limited space up there. You've got to set it up before you even attempt to start the chainsaw, and cover every conceivable aspect of what might happen – and things do happen up there. If you wear the right protective clothing, and follow the guidelines for the procedure of climbing, you'll never have an accident because it's been made so safe. Basically, think safety all the time. Think of your ground crew if you're dropping branches. I remember one fellow, when all the elms were coming down; it was just before Christmas, and a small pole came down and hit him and broke his jaw. He had to have it wired up and spent Christmas sucking whisky through a straw!'

MR. H.'s ELM COMES TO TOWN TO GIVE FESTIVAL A VIEW

"DAILY MIRROR" REPORTER

JUST where the Bailey Bridge ends on the South Bank site of the Festival of Britain is a hole.

The hole goes down 15ft, where a wharf building once stood, and before it was dug various people spent eighteen months discussing it.

For this is no ordinary hole, but the new home of Mr. Hillier's zelcova acuminata.

Fifty years ago he planted the seed in a pleasant spot at his nursery in West Hill, Winchester.

And from it grew a zelcova, known simply as a water elm. A landscape architect decided it was just the tree to decorate the South Bank.

Down at the nursery today the gardeners will start digging round the roots of the 40ft. high elm.

Tomorrow a crane will lift out the ten tons of elm, with almost two tons of soil, and over the week-end the tree, packed in straw, will be driven to the South Bank.

Sixty-eight more water elms from other nurseries will follow the first to the South Bank. Even more will decorate the new London County Council Lansbury housing site at Poplar, and the Festival Gardens at Battersea. A Festival spokesman said yesterday: "The transplanting will be a tricky job.

"We have had expert advice and must now go ahead because the South Bank restaurant and the end of the bridge cannot be completed until the first tree is in position."

The present Mr. Hillier said: "The water elm was chosen as the ideal tree as it will show well in the view across the Thames, and its height will set off the Festival buildings.

"I have been up and had a look at the hole and it should do very well indeed. The bomb rubble at the bottom will be useful for drainage. Zelcova is a tree that likes its drink in moderation."

Eric George, now retired, was responsible for hauling the 40-foot water elm to the South Bank, London, in 1950

Post-war years found Britain in jubilant mood, and in 1951 the Festival of Britain got on its way. It was described in the programme of the South Bank Exhibition as 'one united act of national re-assessment, and one corporate reaffirmation of faith in the nation's future'. Battersea Park in London became the Festival Pleasure Gardens. For many it meant days of joyous celebration, but others worked hard in preparation: Hubert was no exception.

A shuttle service of river boats made it easy to get from the South Bank Exhibition to the Festival Gardens in Battersea Park; a place for the visitor to London to relax. In contrast to the hard surface of London's roads and buildings, trees and plants were placed to give refreshment to the eye. In 1950 there was but one tree on the South Bank site that was once a swamp, but by the time the festival began in 1951, more than sixty had been brought in from the Home Counties. There were water elms, maples, limes and poplars, white beams, birches, a catalpa, a Turkey oak and many others. Hillier Nurseries of Winchester planted a forty foot high water elm weighing ten tons and carrying two tons of soil.

During the festival year, Hubert was responsible for the siting and safety of a steel tree-walk through the branches of eight or so trees near the main avenue of Battersea Park. There is a little of the child in every adult, so it is not surprising that adults as well as children took delight in joining in the adventure of a walk through the treetops. As a tree surgeon, Clive can confirm: 'Fifty foot up a tree is the most peaceful place on earth. I tell you it is, it really is. You can sit there in your harness –

The Tree Walk formed part of the amusements at the Festival Gardens in 1951, to celebrate the Festival of Britain

literally. I used to get them to put my flask of coffee and sandwiches in a bucket and I would pull it up and have my breakfast up in the tree rather than come down again.'

As well as his interest in arboriculture, Hubert always maintained his lifelong love of flowers and plants. There was a shortage of specimen indoor plants after the war and his search for variety took him far and wide, especially for the furnishing of the Royal Festival Hall in 1951. For some plants, more particularly when he wanted citrus trees, he travelled to Italy with a member of Supplies Department who would do the purchasing under his guidance. He found other plants at German shows and, of course, Holland was the favourite place for tulip bulbs. Hubert points out that few people realise that the height to which Dutch tulips of a particular variety grow, varies according to the location they come from. 'A Darwin variety from one area would tower above the same variety from another.' He would therefore have to ensure that the bulbs for a particular scheme all came from the same grower and the same area, as variation could mean having to work out another. He recalls how when the underground trains passed beneath the Embankment gardens, the tulips would vibrate, nodding and shaking their heads in unison as if to be taking part in an elegant ballet!

In his search for large specimen plants, Hubert was invited to the Russian Embassy. This was, indeed, an unusual event in those times. He wonders whether some members of the public really appreciated the efforts made to please them. On one occasion architects suggested that giant cacti would make grand architectural plants; this was an expensive exercise, for the cost of each plant was £35. Nevertheless, it was obviously not respected by some members of the public who carved their initials into the green flesh of the cacti with nail files!

By 1952, all the horticultural features at the Festival Gardens, Battersea, came under Hubert's jurisdiction. He would frequently start work at half-past four in the morning visiting Covent Garden, off the Strand, in search of plants, and at half-past eight in the evening he could still be found working on the bedding plants at Festival Gardens, where he had his own office. He has often been described as a workaholic, but says, 'It did not feel like hard work because I was so interested in doing those things.'

Hubert had enjoyed collecting plants ever since he was a lad; and it was in this pursuit that he had had an exciting adventure when visiting Italy in his teens on a student exchange. He was staying at Villa Hanbury at La Mortola Garden on the

border of France and Italy, where plant-hunting expeditions set off to go up into the mountains. At that time the mountains were heavily guarded, and there were electric fences and floodlights marking the boundaries. Those intending to climb the mountains were advised to consult with the commander, to give their route and gain permission before embarking upon their journey. But boys will be boys, and Hubert and his Scots friend ignored this advice and set off on a search firstly for particular species of *campanula*; also to see holly ferns, a species which Hubert's father had known in Cumbria and which was then becoming a rarity; and *soldanella*, which has the power to melt snow when pushing its way through. However, it wasn't long before the two fellows found themselves under shellfire. They were stopped by the army, who snatched their botanical books and drawings and declared they were spies with coded diagrams. The two lads, who could not communicate in a foreign language, were swiftly marched back at bayonet point and had rather a frightening time until they were released some hours later.

Hubert continued to collect British plants, and fifty years after he had left Kew, he had a fine collection of almost a thousand pressed specimens. They were much admired and gained a memorial award at Kew, but over the years many deteriorated and Hubert reduced the collection to about four hundred. In 1991 he presented them to the University of Reading and offered to clean them up. They accepted the collection gladly, but refused his offer to clean them: 'We want all you've got' they assured him. In fact they wanted to carry out tests for industrial deposits accumulated during the previous sixty or seventy years. This was a pleasing factor which had never occurred to Hubert, but which he considered an added bonus of some value.

Nowadays, Hubert enjoys his memories and is happy to surround himself with garden books and the memorabilia of his sixty-eight years in the horticultural industry. His shelves are lined with garden books, and on the walls of his sitting-room he has a collection of plates depicting British flora; there are photographs taken during his long career, and last, but not least, are his well deserved medals. The MBE was gained for his London County Council activities in the parks and woodlands of Greater London, and for the high horticultural standard of the Festival Gardens and the South Bank during the fifties and sixties. A gold medal was bestowed by the Royal Forestry Society and the Associate of Honour medal awarded by the Royal Horticultural Society for services to horticulture. There was also an award from the Arboricultural Association, of which he was a founder member, for 'services to arboriculture'.

Hubert can be justly proud that he started out as 'a practitioner of gardening, a tiller of the soil, and finishing up as a respected professional', teaching others new methods which he himself had developed. He is also happy with the knowledge that his son Clive is enjoying an outdoor life and the practical skills of arboriculture, and benefiting from the practices that he himself put into operation. He gives praise to members of staff, officers and workers who worked alongside him at all stages of his career. 'Without such co-operation and friendship life would have been very dull, and without a good deputy and supervisors, impossible.'

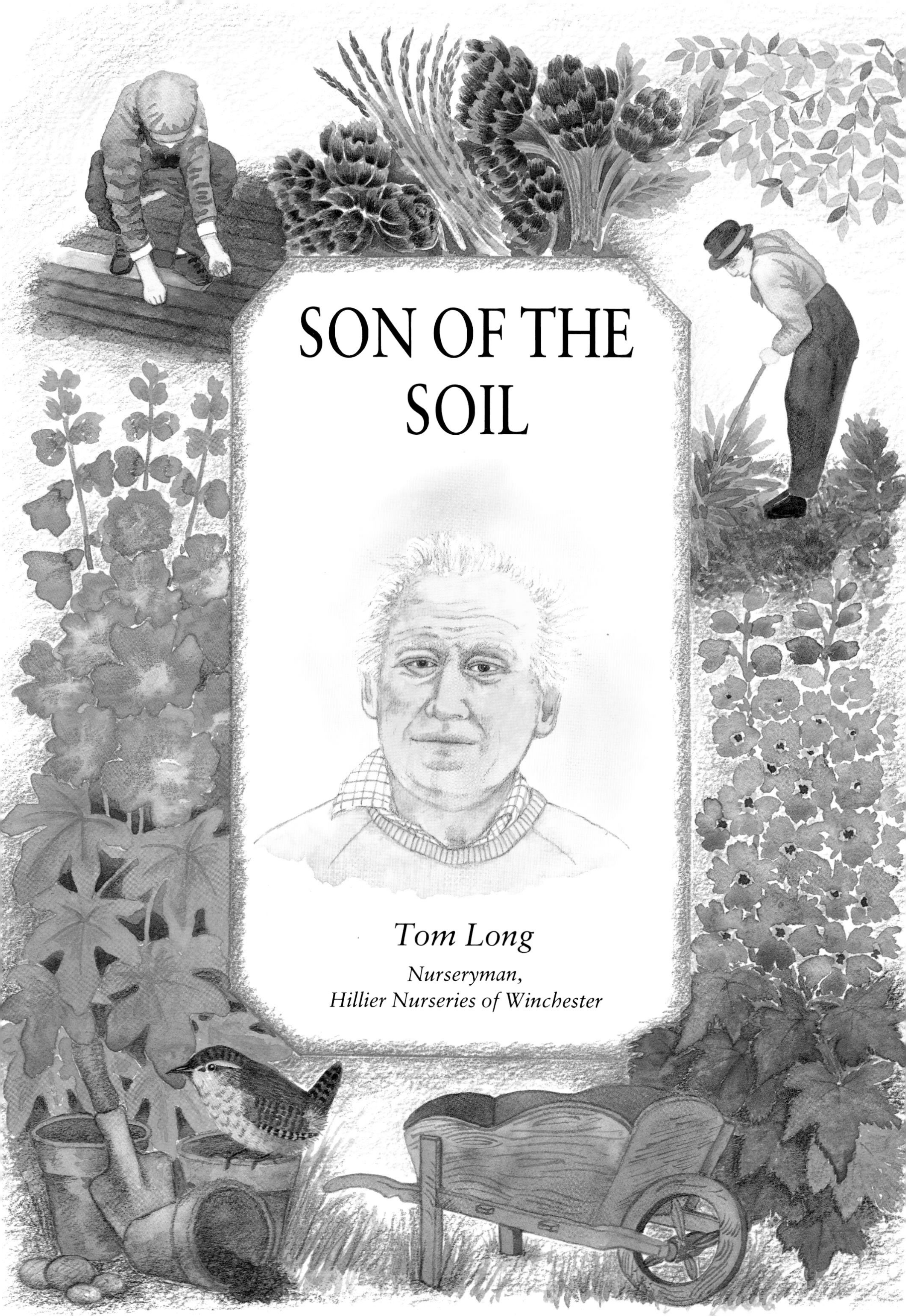

SON OF THE SOIL

Tom Long

Nurseryman,
Hillier Nurseries of Winchester

Tom Long was born in Winchester in 1936 and grew up during the war. His family were ardent supporters of the 'Dig for Victory Campaign' and they all looked forward with enthusiasm to the regular weekend expeditions made to their allotments. Tom's mother and grandmother would pack up picnics and the whole family would go off to enjoy a day's gardening and doing their bit for their country. Tom and his brothers all developed a profound interest in plants and gardens; Tom, however, was the only one to take up gardening as a profession: 'I didn't look at the money side, I didn't really take any interest in how much it was paying at the time, although now I sometimes wish I had done.'

When leaving school, Tom applied to Hillier Nurseries for his first job and has been with them ever since, except for the compulsory period of National Service. He started at Hillier's Saint Cross Nursery, Ghost Corner, on the 1 January 1952. There was no bank holiday in those days, and some say the first day of the year became a bank holiday because so many people were late for work, or did not appear at all, staying at home to recover from the revelry of heralding in the New Year.

However, Tom arrived on the dot of twenty-past seven, after a long bicycle ride in the cold from his home in Winchester. He reported to the foreman, Mr Woodland, and was put to work tending herbaceous, alpine and water plants. 'I got to like the herbaceous and alpines because that was the section I was put on. It does grow on you,' laughed Tom in his usual jovial manner.

Looking back, Tom considers himself fortunate in that he was allowed to spend several years at one crop, and was therefore able to get to know herbaceous plants well. 'Now, if I pick up an herbaceous plant, I'll smell the root and people will say, "What are you doing that for?" It's amazing how many different herbaceous plants, even Michaelmas daises, have a different smell to the root. Perhaps when it was dormant and you were lifting, you'd reassure yourself you were lifting the right side of the label. I remember the "Ballards"; they stuck out quite well as having a different smell to the root. Not many people do this, but I still do. It's the same with the iris, the orris root, it's quite distinct, and the Gladwyn iris, which you find in the hedgerows in Dorset.'

Through the winter, time was spent lifting orders, and then the herbaceous plants had to be split and laid in for spring planting. In those days everything was dug by hand, and hand-planted. If it was a really big field, Hillier's might use their plough and harrow and it would be dug by hand afterwards. After 1953 a rotavator was used, but plants continued to be dug in by hand.

'There were usually about a dozen garden staff – Mr Woodland and his assistant, Martin Drew, about six blokes dealing with the herbaceous field planting, three in the greenhouses, and there would be a specialist propagator. That was all very cloak and dagger in those days and you would have to do so many years before you could get in on propagation.' The girls did the lighter work and were kept occupied in the alpine section where they would handle only 3in pots, that is 7cm today.

Tom Long enjoyed his work with plants and being in the open air. 'They weren't a bad crowd of people. In those days they were more happy with their lot and most of them were doing the thing they wanted to do.' He does feel that Hillier's staff were perhaps a very insular crowd of people. 'They knew themselves to be the best nursery in the country, and then the staff of each department took such pride in its work that a great feeling of competition between themselves was generated.' Tom's was 'Number 3 Nursery' and they considered themselves the best on the firm. The competitive spirit meant that each department did its best to keep its nursery at the top, and the firm seemed to foster this *esprit de corps*.

H.G. Hillier (later Sir Harold, and affectionately known by the staff as H.G.) was the boss in those days, and although his presence was rare, he engendered an aura of authority befitting a person of seniority. In turn, the employee knew he must obey a certain code of behaviour.

'You did not leave a mess behind you, and you knew you had to keep yourself tidy. It was expected of you and it was all part of that generation. You had come through a war so you did not waste things; things were still hard to come by. If you had a tear in your trousers you had it sewn up – your mother saw to that – so that they lasted a bit longer and you were tidy for work.'

When Tom came upon one of H.G.'s catalogues he felt he was part of something big, but was not really clear what this was. 'When my old neighbour asked me, after I'd been there for a few months, "Are you going to Chelsea?" I did not even know that Chelsea was the Royal Horticultural Society Flower Show. So I went and asked and was told: "One day when you know a bit you will be able to go." So, to get to go, you had to show willing and keenness that you were interested in the job. You just did not get picked if you were passing the day along and worked with your clothes torn and that sort of thing.'

Tom went to Winchester home-base nursery in the winter when it snowed; that was the garden centre now opposite the county hospital. 'They did house-plants, bedding plants, chrysanthemums and so on, and we helped them prepare for the following spring. Sometimes we did planting and because it was cold we would cover the ground with straw overnight and rake it off in the morning ready for carrying on the next day's work.' Now with hindsight, Tom thinks this was a very slow operation compared with modern times.

'Sometimes we were sent up to the shop in Winchester High Street where they weighed their own flower and vegetable seeds. There would be two or three of us weighing up eighths of an ounce of seeds from a hundredweight sack of carrot seeds. It's grammes today, but then it was ounces. You would have a spell at that and while you were there, they would show you how to do a bit of wreath work, making holly wreaths at Christmas, or if it was Mothering Sunday time, making sprays. Occasionally they would send you out with the bike delivering to local customers; that was to save the van going.'

In those days they used to start lifting the water lilies in late spring when the water was warming up and the leaves were forming. There were paths nine inches wide

Hillier's shop at 95 High Street, Winchester, where Tom Long weighed up seeds and learned to do 'floral work' (Hillier Nurseries)

between the tanks, and it was Tom's job to make up the baskets with wire-netting and line them with turf to stop the roots going into the water:

'One day, it was just before twelve o'clock, and Martin Drew, the under-foreman, and myself were doing the orders for water lilies and getting the baskets ready. I turned to him and said "Which one?" and he said "That one in the next pond". I put my foot out on what I thought was the path, and of course, it wasn't – it was just a leaf, and I went in up to here!' Tom drew his hand across his neck.

'The old fellow in the packing-shed looked over and he told the foreman I did it on purpose so that I could have an extra hour for dinner, because I would have to go home and get a change of clothes. But I can assure you I didn't!'

When Tom started work, the hours had just come down from a 47- to a 46-hour week. They started at 7.10am in the summer time and finished at 5pm, and on Saturdays at midday. In winter time, when there was no light, they started at 7.20am but they had to make up the time, and could opt either to have less time for dinner or to work longer on Saturdays. Tom opted for the shorter dinner hour as he played football for the Winchester league on Saturdays. His wage at fifteen, when he was still living at home, was £2 16s a week, and he qualified for the agricultural wage increases each year. In later years he enjoyed the extra money that was 'the right of a man travelling the shows', but the men would be questioned as to why they thought they were worth more.

H.G. Hillier, now remembered for the greatly renowned Hillier Arboretum, Ampfield, near Romsey in Hampshire that he started in January 1955, was extremely industrious. He did not work by a clock: 'He used to say that he worked twenty-four hours a day' but Tom remembers 'When we got a bit older we used to say, "Well, you're getting the money, aren't you? We're not!" H.G. did not have too much contact with the staff because his catalogues, notebooks and collecting plants took a hell of a lot of time. He relied on his foremen to run the departments, and usually all they got was a message on the back of an envelope, to save a new piece of paper. That was his filing system. When you think of the range of plants we had – and although we still have a big range, it's not so big as it was – and that man was doing it without a computer. Just think, he was doing it manually on rough paper and odd notebooks! If he lost one of those, it was something to lose – where a cutting had come from, who sent it, what date it was. He seemed to will a cutting to take, because it was the only one to have been given to him.'

When Tom came out of the army he had no intention of going back to the same job, but then he took a bike ride out into the country and came across Hillier's new herbaceous and alpines nursery, and was invited to take his job back. He says if he had ridden off in the other direction he would not be where he is now. 'They had grown and had got up to twelve acres of herbaceous plants, and supplied the shop with flowers for weddings and so on. Now they have an even larger organised programme of selling flowers. Yes, everything had got bigger. There was a packing shed, they had gone over to rotavators, and they were doing their own shows. They also had a bulb catalogue and potted up a lot of spring bulbs; there was a bulb store in the old stable at one stage. They did about five thousand bulbs, and after the flowers

A group of staff in 1932. Sir Harold Hillier remembered the 'good old days' thus: 'I remember the days when my father, my uncle and the staff worked from 6am to 6pm, finishing at 4pm on Saturdays, using hurricane lamps in the winter, early mornings and evenings. In the days of Shroner, this meant a walk of six miles before 6am. Only if one was lucky was there a lift in a wagon. After a high tea, my father would work in the office at the back of 95 High Street, returning home in time for bed at 11.30pm.' (Hillier Nurseries)

had been cut off, they were sold off very cheaply as mixed bulbs. It did not seem much, but it saved them going on the bonfire heap.

'The department had gone up to about fifteen, with the girls still working in alpines. The girls had to use the toilets of the local householders, but they didn't mind – it was a chance to have a cup of tea with their friends.'

In the sixties Tom took a job as foreman in the landscaping department. He enjoyed the work because it got him out and about meeting people. He did all sorts of landscape work, 'from gardens for old ladies to that one in the park where the parks' superintendents stood on their brooms watching you, you know.' One job was at Winchester College, where the art master had initiated a fund from amongst the old Wykehamists as he thought there was not enough planting being done for future generations: he raised £800 to be spent on its development. At that time Tom was earning about £8 a week, so £800 seemed a lot of money to him then. They planted a lot of unusual trees around the old college buildings and cloisters and the sports fields. On the edge of the cricket field at Garnier Road they planted five *Cercis siliquastrum*, (the 'Judas tree', so-called because it is the species from which Judas is said to have hanged himself), and they are there to this day.

Tom and his team did a variety of landscaping jobs around the country. He would take a few men in his car, because not many people had a car in those days, and they would leave in a gang at five o'clock in the morning and would not get back until nine o'clock at night. One client, Mr Leighton, the optician at Hove, was particularly pleased with them and wanted them to enjoy themselves. He encouraged them to have plenty of time to eat and drink, and when they were finished he invited them to stay longer. 'You don't have to rush. Get a bit of overtime – I'm paying the bill!' he said.

Tom's last landscaping job was a big one at Christchurch for the town council. They had demolished a lot of old houses and made a traffic island, and instead of just grassing it over or planting it with heathers, asked Hillier's to landscape it.

'The winter of 1961, it was, and it was hard work! They had made the island of reclaimed sewage sludge that had been sterilised, and it was on a steep slope. They put the soil on the island without any supervision and they had dumped it all on the bottom of the slope. It was a wet month, and when we went to start, a load of it had to be brought up the slippery slope on planks to get the site firm and ready for planting. One day H.G. came down and helped build the rockeries himself.'

Tom made a request to remain permanently on landscape work, and even thought about moving to a landscaping firm. However, in 1961 he married and the move was forgotten, and he went back to 'herbaceous' and became involved with 'Shows'.

Tom has worked at three Chelsea Flower Shows. In those days they had separate stands for shrubs, roses, herbaceous and alpines inside the tent, and one year Harold Hillier also organised a stand of hollies in the avenue outside. 'They used about 150 different varieties of hollies. That was when Roy Lancaster joined Hillier's and he helped run this. It would be a different genus of plants each year.' Tom enjoyed show-work, and found it not so much hard as tiring.

The men would design the stands between them. At the provincial shows they would do a stand of cut flowers some thirty feet long; preparation for the Chelsea Flower Show, however, would be more rigorous. Potted plants were put on show there, specially raised and started early in the previous autumn.

'Some would have to go in the freezer, some didn't. Some in the full shade, some put out in the full sun. I never pulled my hair out, there was no point because you couldn't always make them bloom, and if they didn't come out you couldn't use them. There's a lot of camouflage goes on at a stand. Something may not have leaves on, but it can have a good flower stalk, so you camouflage the fact.

'It was work, eat and sleep. There wasn't much time for a joke. Clearing away was far worse than putting up. They sold most things off on Friday night and the public would buy at an inflated price just because it was from Chelsea, but anything still looking good went off to the Bath and West Show that followed on.'

They did summer shows every fortnight around the country. 'A showman's lot is a hard lot, and hard on his wife because he is never home.'

When Tom finished with show-work he took over the herbaceous section, and because the firm had grown so big, they took on a man from Wisley to manage the alpine section. Tom has an apprentice nowadays, and when he last took the boy's papers home to mark he found his spelling was atrocious: 'He writes as he speaks, and even created different hybrids just by bad spelling!'

Queen Mary at Chelsea Flower Show
(Hillier Nurseries)

Together with his team of twelve people, Tom is always busy getting orders 'off the beds and off to the packing sheds'. This is his main job, and he is quite happy to do this until his not-too-distant retirement. 'Every man is dependent upon the man before him doing his job satisfactorily. The packer is dependent upon the propagator and he in turn is dependent upon the cuttings man. If the material is not up to standard, it will be sent back.

'In the old days H.G. would come along with a packet of seeds that perhaps he had collected in Korea. "Raise all you can." "What's all you can?" "Every single one of them, they are gold dust." You didn't know if you were going to sell them. He kept a mystique really, and he sold on mystique. If you had five plants and he brought a party of people round and there was Lord Avon and Lord so-and-so, or perhaps it was a princess, he would play one off against the other. "I'm sorry, I've only got five and Lord Lonsdale said he would like one." In his way he was a good salesman, wasn't he?'

Tom looked thoughtful: 'It's the older generation that generates the money in gardening. Some military people want to put something back into the world that perhaps they feel they have been mangling up. When they were away on their campaigns they must have seen the most wonderful plants. Perhaps at one time they might have pitched their tents amongst magnolia trees. Yes, perhaps they now want to make up for any destruction they may have contributed to.'

Tom also believes there has been a lot of unnecessary desecration of the countryside, particularly with ploughing up of hedges and felling of trees, often without planning permission. '"Capability" Brown, the landscape designer, was responsible for a great deal of destruction in the eighteenth century, but he left gardens for those who came after him and yes, he was moving large trees, even in those days.' Today, Hillier Nurseries are renowned for their work with trees, both raising new stock and transplanting very large specimens, some 200 to 250 years old. 'What started H.G. off, was that he was called in to camouflage aerodromes during the war. They were moving things during the night and they even had their own small-gauge railway for doing it on. The trees were situated around the hangers to disguise them and make them less obvious from the air.

'Winchester chalk was ideal because the soil is only about eighteen inches deep. You only had to go down to this depth and you would hit the pan where the root fibred out, and you could get the winch and pull the tree over and it would break away as clean as a whistle. It's very difficult to move the trees from some types of soil and it cannot be done if the weather is too bad, because as fast as a hole is dug it fills up with water and a pump has to be used to drain it.

'Now Hillier's have an area like a big stony beach, divided into avenues by huge poles concreted into the ground and linked by ships' hawser wires strained to take the weight of the trees; these are usually finished off in one thousand litre pots, which are more convenient. The pots are wire baskets lined with polythene, and to make the job easier, they are filled with potting compost from bags. It's big business! The trees are allowed a minimum of three years to become established and sometimes they are left for several years, and then, when the weather is fine, they are lifted.'

A selection of old Hillier catalogues (Hillier Nurseries)

In the late seventies Harold Hillier started a rare plant unit. There were thousands of varieties of plants and seeds collected abroad and delivered to the nursery, and the job of dealing with them and labelling them was allocated to Tom. In one season he sowed 1,200 different varieties of plants. With all these seeds from all over the world it would have meant so much writing that a number was put on instead. Every plant was coded and listed in a book shared by Tom and Harold Hillier. 'Plants were listed alphabetically and each nursery had a number. Every place, source, plant and seed had a number. The stock on the ground was sectioned and numbered, too.' Tom attended to this task in the evening, when he also made a point of looking up the places the plants had come from. The altitude was also coded and Tom could tell if the specimen could be grown in this country. He was later to find that many plants could be grown on the Isle of Wight that would not grow on the mainland.

In the late sixties Harold Hillier went to the Isle of Wight to give a talk when the

hospital for tuberculosis sufferers at Ventnor was about to be demolished. It had been suggested that the grounds should become a botanic garden, but Harold was not too enthusiastic about the idea and thought it would be better as a sports field. However, the town council contacted him a few months later to say that it had been decided that it *should* become a botanic garden, and would he go over and help. Hillier Nurseries therefore started to shift all their greenhouse stock of Australasian and New Zealand plants – some they donated and others were supplied at a premium rate.

'We were allowed to go there to collect cuttings, and whenever we went to get them we always took a carload of new plants. We'd collect osteospermums, eucalyptus, we'd collect the seed of them *grevilleas*, and South African stuff, *euryops* and so on. It wasn't long before the old stone walls were covered with climbers donated by Hillier Nurseries and other interested people.'

Hillier Nurseries have ceased to visit since the death of Sir Harold Hillier. 'We don't grow so much Australasian stuff now. He was a different chap when he was there. He always used to go over on a Thursday and stay with a relative and I would meet him with the head propagator on a Monday morning at the boat and he would drive us down to Ventnor. We would go and get the cuttings and that. When he was about the garden in the day he became a down-to-earth type of man on those occasions. He enjoyed it. The first time we were there, it got to ten o'clock and the head gardener said, "Come on Hillier, it's cup o' tea time." "Ooh, no time for that," he replied. Then it was three o'clock. Well, after the first time, he looked forward to going to tea. We took three men over once and they were frightened when he said to them "Come on, what kind of cake do you want? Do you want a doughnut, do you want a cream bun, or do you want an ice-cream?" When he'd gone they said, "Oh, we didn't like to say yes!" He said to me once "*You* had a cake with me, Long, what's the matter with those others, aren't I good enough?"'

Tom at work at a Hillier nursery

Sir Harold Hillier died at about the same time as the head gardener retired and another man was brought in from Kew to run the botanic garden, and things changed. They built a grotto and a greenhouse and they made a charge to go into the greenhouse. Unfortunately, the national press has reported that a great deal of pilfering of plants goes on at the botanic gardens, even from the greenhouse, but Tom is sad to say that this has always been something of a problem with gardens opened to the public. 'It's pilfering to order – what is being pinched is for somebody's collection. I found this in the nursery at one time. Somebody said to me "Would you leave the gate open at night?" And I am talking about a really rich person. "Would half-a-crown be enough?" That was when it was half-a-crown, now twelve and a half pence. I told him to get lost. He was a *sempervivum* expert and we had a good collection on the alpine section and there was half-a-dozen varieties he wanted. In them days they were 2s 6d each and he was prepared to come back and filch them! But it wasn't worth worrying the old boy about it, else he would have had us all standing guard at nights. This is why gardens are numbering plants and not naming them nowadays. It's sad, isn't it?'

Tom says he does not worry over things, he switches off when he goes home. He might read his books on plants, but he says this is being switched off. At work he is content to go on meeting orders, so long as he can depend on the men behind doing their bit and the men in front having enough pallets ready for him to fill. Nevertheless, he looks forward to the day when he retires because there are so many things he wants to do. Who knows, perhaps he will get around to putting that stuffed koala bear in the eucalyptus tree in his garden, and when the men come out of the nearby inn, The Potter's Heron, they will see what could be described as the alternative to pink elephants!

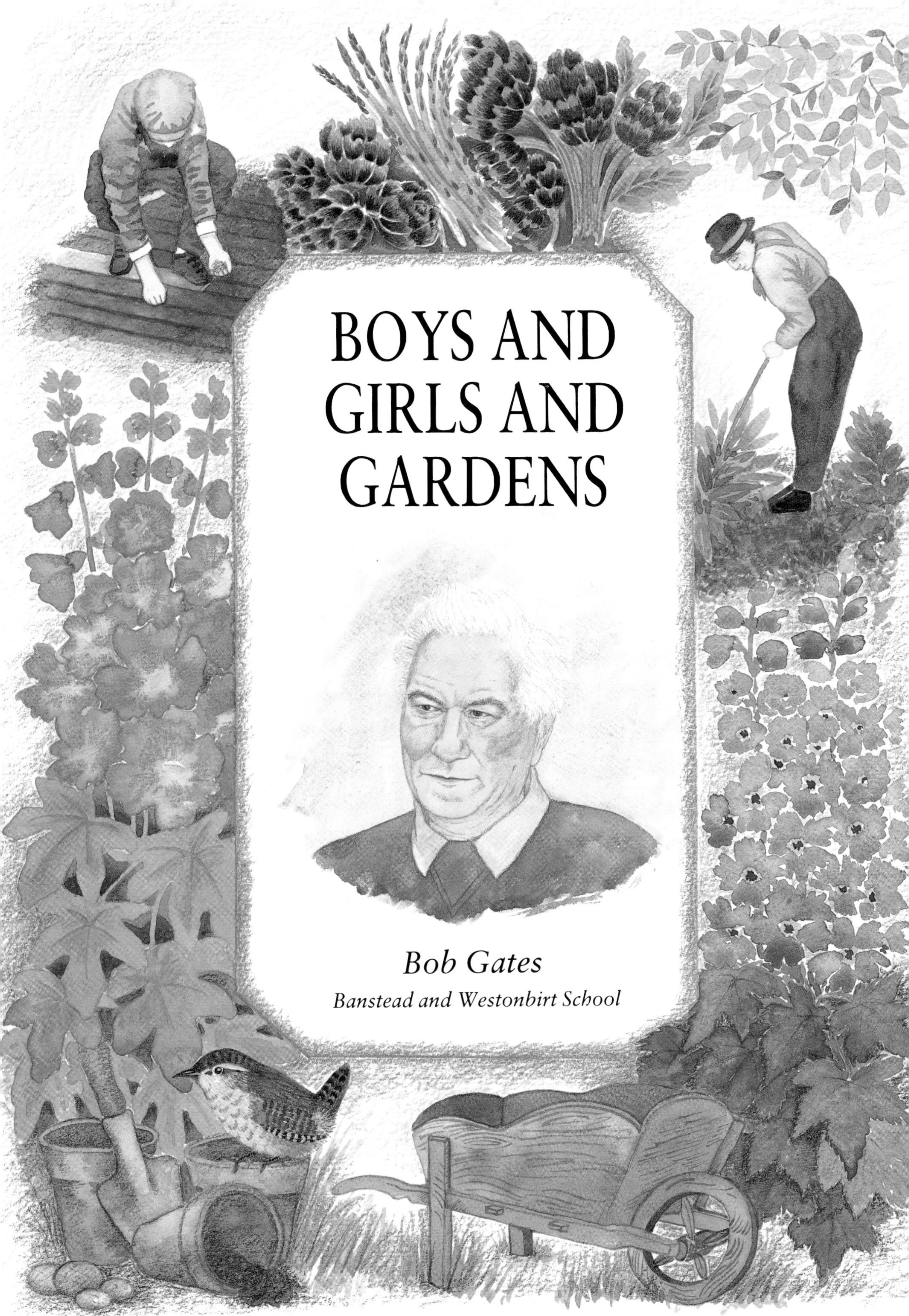

BOYS AND GIRLS AND GARDENS

Bob Gates

Banstead and Westonbirt School

Bob Gates first taught gardening to boys in an approved school at Banstead, then moved to Westonbirt School for girls where he spent most of his career. Bob's father had had a horticultural contracting business in Liverpool, after being in the navy; he was called up again before the outbreak of war in 1938. Bob left school in 1940 and found a number of jobs, before joining the Navy himself in 1943.

When the war ended, Bob joined the staff on the estate in Charlbury of O.V. Watney, the brewer, starting at the bottom as glasshouse journeyman. The head gardener was Mr Buckle. 'There was always great competition between him and the nurserymen at Cirencester about growing cyclamen – they used to vie with each other to get the best plant. Mr Buckle even used to lock the potting-shed door so that you couldn't see what he was putting into the compost! He used to look after the cyclamen as if they were babies, you know.

'Mr Buckle used to grunt instead of saying good morning and after about three weeks I had had enough of this. So the next morning I went "Hrmph". "What did you say Robert? You didn't say good morning." "Well," I said, "I thought that was the way you wanted to be spoken to." He stumped away, but he always said good morning after that.'

Fuel was very short after the war, and consisted mostly of wood. They started to grow quite a lot of tomatoes in pots, to Mrs Watney's disgust, as previously they had produced tropical plants like bananas and pineapples, guavas, cotton and ginger. These were grown in a stove house, which was almost like a botanical garden, but because of the fuel shortages they had to change the produce they grew. There was three-quarters of an acre of greenhouses. 'We used to put a sheet down under the vines and thin the grapes out with scissors, then they used to sell them to the bakers for gooseberry tarts. You couldn't tell the difference! The earliest gooseberry tarts in Charlbury were really grapes! I used to pinch a few grapes sometimes, and the head gardener came up to me one day and said "Look, if you want to steal grapes, take a

BY APPOINTMENT
TO H.M KING
GEORGE V,
H.M. QUEEN
ALEXANDRA,
H.M. THE LATE
KING EDWARD VII.

Experts in the construction and planting of

ROCK GARDENS :: :: DUTCH GARDENS
WATER GARDENS ITALIAN GARDENS
FORMAL GARDENS JAPANESE GARDENS

PULHAM & SON

GARDEN CRAFTSMEN

71 NEWMAN STREET, OXFORD STREET,

LONDON, W.1

GARDEN ORNAMENTS

in "PULHAMITE" STONE.

FIGURES :: SUNDIALS
BIRD BATHS :: VASES
FOUNTAINS :: :: ETC.

LISTS ON RECEIPT OF REQUIREMENTS.

NURSERIES ... BISHOP'S STORTFORD
WORKS ... BROXBOURNE.

tip from me, always use scissors, then I won't know. When you pull them off, I can see the little bits hanging down."'

In the old days the men used to do all the flower decorations in the house – it is a fairly new idea to get girls to come in and do them under contract. At Charlbury the greenhouses were a long way away, so they used to have a horse and cart to take all the cut flowers and pots to the house; cherries and lilies for instance, would be forced in pots. Bob learnt decorating in a grand manner from the head gardener. 'They had carpets of *Cyclamen hederifolium* at Charlbury over the autumn and spring, and the secretary there came out one day and picked loads of these things and put them in little paste jars. O.V. Watney was absolutely furious.' It wasn't 'done' to pick flowers without asking, and the paste jars were completely inappropriate.

They had a nuttery at Charlbury, rare today, which was never mown. In the spring it was absolutely beautiful, full of wild flowers which were indigenous to the area; although Bob feels that an artificial wild garden such as that at Highgrove is very difficult to maintain.

After this practical training at Charlbury, Bob moved to another private estate before going to Wisley as a student. He considered it to be excellent training. Bob had enjoyed his sport in his leisure times at Wisley and decided that he wanted the opportunity to continue, and to find a job which would involve looking after sports grounds.

In fact the job he obtained was as instructor at Banstead Hall, at Banstead in Surrey. It was a short-term approved school catering for about eighty boys aged fourteen to eighteen, and Bob liked it when he got there. There were cricket and football pitches to look after, and Bob played sport every day. Physically the boys were worked very hard. 'If they were on punishment, they couldn't go out, and I used to have them all. I've had as many as seventeen or twenty boys in a line with spades, digging. And people used to come and watch. We had this huge field across the road from the school, and people used to like watching: the ground was going over like a plough, you see, because they were all in line, one behind the other, which was the old-fashioned way of digging – they went across the field. Of course you shoved the lazy ones in the middle, so they'd get their feet chopped off if they didn't keep moving. It was lovely to see this soil just going over, like ploughing. I believed in digging for them, some of these chaps were big and strong, they wanted something to prove themselves, and they didn't mind the digging. You would always have at least six or seven and they were competing all the time. When I left they went and bought a machine, which spoilt the point of the thing.

'The boys were there for attempted murder and things like that. Mainly they were East End lads. Great youngsters, great sense of fun. The approved school system in that day [1949] was based on the public school system of points and houses. Smoking out of hours meant losing four points right away. And there were other things, too: if they lost twelve points in a fortnight then their pocket money would be reduced, and they wouldn't be allowed home at the end of the fortnight. If I caught them, I would say, "take your pick, four points off, or a clock across the backside". But there was no animosity, it was finished with and they could go on. Of course I got reported for it, but they still sent me all the difficult rag-tags. You couldn't do it today, now they have called the analysts in. Mind you, you have all these different drugs today. I used to like the East Enders, they have a great sense of humour, and they make jolly good gardeners, too. We used to have plant diaries just like we did at Wisley – twenty-one plants out on the bench on a Monday morning. They would come in and look at them, and write down what they thought they were. They were good at remembering them, the common names, not in the Latin so they didn't lose interest.'

Under instruction they grew all the vegetables that the school used, and lots of fruit too, such as blackcurrants, which they bottled. They looked after the greenhouse. They also had a hundred varieties of apples, and won prizes with them. Flowers were grown for the local florists. In due course Bob became a senior instructor, and he also met and married his wife Joy while at Banstead.

In 1958 Bob went to Westonbirt School as head gardener, and he stayed for more than thirty years till he retired in 1991. The house at Westonbirt is huge, in the florid high-Victorian manner, and the gardens are superb. The Westonbirt Arboretum, which is open to the public, is just across the road and is managed quite separately, although the wealthy Holford family started the collections of plants in both places.

'I didn't find it too awe-inspiring. Though I didn't like the building at the start. In the bad weather it looks like Alcatraz. Once the sun comes out it's transformed, with those gorgeous browny, creamy, orange shades; it grew on you. The garden is very under-rated, I think. It was designed for a lot of people. It was on the grand scale. To see it you must go up into Holford's sitting-room. Then you see what the grand design is. It was designed to have leisurely walks and little surprises.'

This is the third house at Westonbirt, and before it was completed in 1872, R.S. Holford had already started on the garden design which we can see today. Formal lawns and terraces lead down to the fountain pool, with views across the ha-ha, which hides the road, to the farmland beyond. The other axis leads from the church to the dell with its pond and statue of Mercury. A knot garden, pergola walk and an Italian Garden with architectural features complete the more formal eastern side of the property. The west provides a more informal aspect, with irregular clumps of trees, a lake, grotto and rockery. R.S. Holford was a pioneer collector of trees, shrubs and flowers from around the world, and Sir George continued his interests with a particular penchant for orchids and exotics. At one time three thousand amaryllis were grown in the hothouses, and his camellias were famous.

Bob Gates never wanted to be a working head gardener. He was a 'Head Gardener', a manager of the thirteen men under him, in the mode of the old private gardens where he had started his training. 'Head gardeners were very important people, they were gods. They were very respected and the boss would consult the head gardener on anything and everything. Of course coming to Westonbirt you had a

Westonbirt House

lot of people who didn't realise that the head gardener was really something in his trade. The teachers didn't recognise the head gardener as anything other than an outside worker. I would never succumb to this, so I wasn't always very popular. I always got on well with the headmistresses and the bursars. And the men, we discussed things every day, we didn't have problems there.

'Running a place like that wasn't like running an ordinary garden. The garden itself was twenty-two acres; with all the school sports grounds, and twenty-four grass tennis courts, a hundred and fifty acres in all. We used to mow a hundred acres a week. Also, the golf course became more popular. When I came you could fire a shotgun up every fairway and you wouldn't hit anything – now you'd have a job to get round it on a Sunday afternoon. We made a lot of money on the golf course, and that helped pay for the garden.'

As time went on of course men retired, and mechanisation became more prevalent. When Bob left, he had only three men to help him instead of the original thirteen. 'Strimmers revolutionised Westonbirt because of all that edging – we had two miles of edging altogether. It used to take a man the best part of three days to do the Italian Garden alone with clippers. It took two hours with a strimmer! And electric hedge clippers – though I still think that hand-clipping a hedge with shears is more accurate if you want to do it really well. The others are so quick, you know, even if you put up a string or little guides. You can make a better job with shears. But we don't have many hedges at Westonbirt.'

Bob thinks that he had one of the first strimmers, which was an electric one run off

A view of the gardens

a generator. 'Innovations in machinery came from America, and amateurs had them first. In the early days some of the engines were terrible, we were always repairing them. But the new ones are superb, worth every penny. I never think machinery is expensive. If you had a strimmer, you needed a certain amount of skill, but it gave you more time to do the more skilful jobs.'

There were four men in the kitchen garden and two in the greenhouses. 'In the prospectus of the school in the 1950s, it was said that they grew their own vegetables. One of the Lyons family (the catering people) wanted his daughter to come to Westonbirt, and I took him round the kitchen garden and showed him that we did actually grow them. We used to buy main-crop potatoes, but grow everything else. Miss Scott-Smith, who was the headmistress when I went, asked me why we didn't grow peas and beans. Mind you, I hadn't been there five minutes. "Well, I don't know", I said, "perhaps it's the shelling of them." "Never mind about that," she said, "I'll get the sixth-formers to shell them." And they did for a bit!'

Bob used to sell the surplus produce in Tetbury and Malmesbury. Marketing by head gardeners was a practice probably started during the war, and in Bob's opinion it ruined a good number of private gardens when it continued after the war. The owners might have no idea of marketing, and the traders would come in and take all the best. Or the owner would give away all the choicest flowers to her friends, leaving the head gardener unable to make the garden pay, as he should have done. In the end Bob stopped the practice at Westonbirt. He also stopped his staff from making wreaths and hanging baskets because his men were making items for the florists and funeral directors at a price which was simply not viable.

Bob sold about five thousand Christmas trees a year. 'I used to have this lovely lady, a didicoy, a dealer – Mrs Hughes, very rich, but she couldn't write. She was very good, she used to take all the roots out when she lifted the trees; if you just cut them off, the ground with the roots in is no good to anyone. She used to come with all these notes. The one year her daughter came when her mother wasn't well, and she wrote me a cheque. One year the Governors wanted a higher price for the trees, and so I went to Mrs Hughes, she went higher but couldn't go any more, and I thought she was quite right not to pay more. So I stopped doing it. Pity. It was an income coming in from ragland, and the school used a fair number of the trees, too. She was as honest as the day was long, that woman. She was strictly on the line.'

Amongst the more unusual trees they have on the estate is one of the oldest and largest metasequoias in Britain. They also had the largest sugar maple, although this has gone now; and an *Aesculus turbinata* grows on the lawn which is supposed to be the very one which A.J. Bean used for his drawing of the species in his well known book *Trees and Shrubs Hardy in the British Isles*. Bob used to grow some trees from seed and tried to keep the garden as it was, according to A. Bruce Jackson's 1927 catalogue on Westonbirt. Sometimes Bob found it difficult to get the old varieties, which are now defunct; and the new and probably smaller varieties which have been developed are not always suitable for the size of Westonbirt. 'The house is so huge, it needs something to bring it down. We had the first *Gleditsia triacanthos*, the soap tree. The form you see a lot is *inermis*, or "Sunburst". There were two planted at the same time, one at Kew. The Westonbirt one just got better and better. It used to have fruit like laburnum. Apparently it was used years ago as soap in Japan. Lovely tree, very feathery.' Bob never burnt leaves in autumn. Instead he raked them up and put them in the covers, the irregular clumps of trees which are dotted around the lawns. There they rotted down and provided food for birds and wildlife.

The lake is a feature of the garden: 'It was part of the design. On the very old maps there were ponds for the vicarage there. Then when they built the present house, the lake was put here for a very good reason, because you get the reflection of the house in the lake when it's full. It's very well thought out. Anyway, the lake got algae in there – it made a blanket. It used to bubble up from the bottom. Terrible! We cleaned the lake out, scrubbed it, filled the holes. The water authorities couldn't give us any information. The water was high in oxygen. They suggested rainbow carp to eat the algae, which they did, but they couldn't eat it fast enough. The lake is built on the old riverbed, and the river is now culverted. When it was made, it would have been made with puddled clay. This was built on streams, and in 1870-something they had to concrete it – the date is on the bottom of the lake. But in 1975 we had those tremendous floods, and I reckon these just scoured the old river out. The lake bed is hollow underneath, and I reckon myself that all the effluent is lying there and just seeping up, particularly as the concrete is getting old.' (In fact the lake has recently been cleaned out and repaired and so it is clear once again.)

'I wouldn't let the girls do anything. One of the biggest problems we had at Westonbirt were the sticks coming down from the trees. You couldn't mow without

The Mercury Pool at Westonbirt

picking them up and it all had to be done by hand. We had a great storm one time and a tremendous lot came down. I mentioned it to the bursar of the day. Next thing was, "I've got it all fixed," he said. "I'm going to have all these girls picking up things." "Who is going to be in charge of them? I'm not!" You've never seen such a thing in all your life, fifty or sixty girls all walking round with one stick each. We had more to do clearing up after them! And you can't blame them – their dads weren't paying £3,000 a year for them to be lackeys, were they? I used to tell the girls to sit down and enjoy the view. They were very conscious of the gardens. But I used to make them clean up if they smoked, that was the only thing.

'I honestly can't think of any vandalism from the girls. There was litter sometimes, I used to tell Mrs O'Brien in the tuck shop that there were a lot of sweetie papers in the Italian Garden and she used to shut the shop till they had all been cleaned up! They used to decorate the Mercury statue sometimes. I used to come down of a morning and there he'd have a bra on, a hat and a boot on his foot, and lipstick. I used to leave it till they had taken their photographs!' For a while the junior girls had small gardens to work themselves, but this did not prove very satisfactory in the long run, and the area is now a flowery sun-trap designed by Bob.

Sports ground maintenance is very expensive, and particularly for a place such as a school, where the use is limited to specific term times. 'I've swept snow off the grass tennis courts so they could play.' The usual practice is for some of the courts to be rested, to allow the base lines to recover while the others are used, but in this case it could not be done, as all the girls played sports every afternoon. So the grounds had

Planting a gleditsia in 1982, to celebrate the 50th anniversary of the Westonbirt Association. Bob Gates is on the left

to take a lot of wear. Too much fertiliser makes the grounds too soft, so that was not a solution at Westonbirt. They did try renting out the sports facilities in the holidays, but then they couldn't control what happened. 'You may spend £7,000 doing your tennis courts, and people come in wearing all sorts of shoes, and when the surface of a hard court is broken, you can't really do anything about it.

'When I first went to Westonbirt, you wouldn't credit it, I used to watch fascinated, because to make the running track they had a couple of sixth form maths girls with a piece of string, the right length, stretching it out and round, and marking it with the tracks. Miss Scott-Smith asked me to make a new track, and we took over doing it then. We had Olympic jumping pits, can you imagine it!'

Bob always wanted to make sports pitches out at the front of the house, which had previously been rough fields for grazing farm animals and horses. When Miss Newton came as headmistress, she was all for it. 'I spent a long time getting water levels and digging holes to discover the drainage and so on.' The work wasn't actually done till much later. Trees had to be felled to make room, though the three cedars immediately in front of the house could not be removed as they had been planted by Queen Mary, Edward VII and Princess Alexandra. 'I think some of the governors made a bit of a hoo-hah about it. They always try to disguise the fact that Westonbirt is a school. They put the swimming pool miles away, nearly into Shoeburyness!' The land in front of the house is now elegantly smooth grass for playing fields.

There used to be herbaceous borders in the Italian Garden, and Bob tried for many years to get rid of the convolvulus. Eventually he suggested that they should put the borders down to grass – after several years of mowing it they would be able to see if the convolvulus was still growing there. If not, it could be restored to herbaceous beds as it was. 'I didn't do anything there, that could not be easily restored.'

Sir George Holford liked daisies in his lawn. However, they don't wear very well in bad weather, and in some weathers they will root from the leaves, and seed like fury. 'I got rid of them. If you weedkill a lawn it would save two mowings, which may not sound a lot, but it gave me time to have men on holiday. Exams made a difference to the mowing. What you don't want is movement – sound doesn't matter, but movement catches a girl's eye. We used to have to turn the birds off! We had to mow at lunchtimes. You had one day of rain and couldn't mow, and then you were never catching up. We were a bit restricted.'

Bob and his men managed grass tennis courts, lacrosse and hockey pitches, the athletics and the golf, and of course the superb Grade 1 listed gardens. English Heritage, the Garden History Society and the National Trust, who came to visit Bob from time to time, were always surprised that he could run Westonbirt with so few staff. Now Bob has retired, and lives with his wife Joy in a cottage filled with his expert wood carvings, many of them carved from trees which Bob once tended at Westonbirt.

Wartime Gardeners

ALLOTMENTS measured 90 x 30ft. In 1939 there were 815,000. By 1943 the Dig for Victory campaign got well on its way and there were 1,400,000 allotments. Gardens were formed all over blitzed cities in parks, on bomb sites, in back yards, on roofs, on top of Anderson shelters, and even in a bomb crater in a courtyard of Westminster Palace.

During World War II boxes of vegetable seed collections of seventeen assorted varieties were sent as gifts to the British people from their friends in America through the British War Relief Society Incorporated, New York.

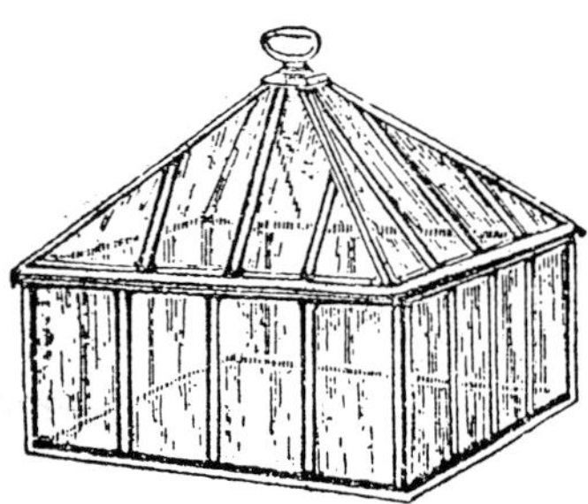

Flora remembers the Land Army

FLORENCE Hutchinson was born near Whitby, Yorkshire, in 1907. She is a happy person with a gentle Yorkshire accent and even her voice seems to smile. She says she loved working in the open air and now she sits outside whenever the weather permits.

Flora, as she is now called, because of her love of flowers, was brought up on the family farm and became a landgirl for Ilkley Council. It was wartime and she preferred to do this rather than go into a factory or join the forces, which were the alternative compulsory occupations for young ladies.

When war broke out in 1939, the nation relied on seventy per cent of its food and livestock feedstuff being imported, thus leaving itself dangerously open to blockade. The target was, therefore, soon set as self-sufficiency. The Women's Land Army came to the fore and by 1943, 87,000 girls were working in fields and gardens.

Flora volunteered early on, because she 'did not want pushing anywhere'. Two million acres were reclaimed during the war in the nation's effort to become self-sufficient, and Flora did her bit. She planted potatoes for the war effort on patches of waste ground:

'One field, it was a grass field, they ploughed it out and we all, there were about four of us, planted potatoes, but we didn't plant them like they do all in rows. It was a bit, well, rather rough. We used to make holes with a dibber and just pop in a potato. Ooh! We had some fun! There was no-one showing us how to do it. There was a superintendent, but he didn't come round much.'

Some men did not give women much credit for their ability to work on the land, so perhaps this is why Flora and her team were left largely to their own devices. Flora and her chums also enjoyed helping in the nurseries growing vegetables and tomatoes. There was a greengrocer's shop in Ilkley that used to buy their produce. Petrol was rationed at this time, but this did not matter to the young ladies. The shop was only ten minutes away and they pushed the produce there on a trolley.

The Women's Land Army

THE Women's Land Army was formed in 1917, disbanded in November 1919 and re-formed in June 1939. At the outbreak of war in 1939, 1,000 volunteers were available for duty and undertook all kinds of work on the land. By June 1944 there were 80,000 women in the Land Army and one third came from towns and cities. They earned less than £3 per week and had one week's holiday a year.

'She milks; she does general farmwork which includes ploughing, weeding, hoeing, dung-spreading, lifting and clamping potatoes and other root crops, brushing and laying hedges, cleaning ditches, haymaking, harvesting, threshing; in more specialised ways, she prunes and sprays fruit-trees, picks and packs the fruit, makes and lays thatch, makes silage, pulls flax, destroys rats, works an excavator, reclaims bad land; works in commercial and private gardens, works in the forest felling timber, measuring timber, planting young trees . . . It is quite an impressive list . . .'

Vita Sackville-West, 1944

Useful Hints and Tips for Land Girls

Remedy for Roughened Hands
Put 1 ounce of olive oil and 1 ounce chopped beeswax into a jar in the oven until melted. Cool and, when easy to handle, roll into a ball. Rub lightly into the hands after washing. A little oat flour will remove greasiness.
Making Shoes Waterproof
Cut up a little beeswax and put into a jar. Cover with a little castor oil or Neat's-foot oil. Stand in a warm place till wax is melted. Stir thoroughly. Allow to cool. If too thick add a little more oil.
To use, warm a little, apply with stiff brush while quite soft. Let that coat harden, warm boots slightly, and apply another coat. Neat's-foot oil alone is quite good.
To Make Gum Boots Slip on and Off Easily
Sprinkle French chalk inside the gum boots from time to time.

from *Land Girl, A Manual for Volunteers in the Women's Land Army*, 1940–46

The Choice

When skies are blue and days are bright
A kitchen garden's my delight,
Set round with rows of decent box
And blowsy girls of hollyhocks . . .

Katherine Tynan, 1915

Potatoes

WHO can have thought, says Roze, in his elaborate Histoire de la Pomme de Terre, that the Potato, having its home in Chile, naturalized in Peru, where it was cultivated from time immemorial, introduced into Europe in the sixteenth century, despised in the seventeenth, slightly esteemed in the eighteenth, would have taken so important a place in commerce and form a subject of abiding interest to almost all nations in the nineteenth century?

Gardeners' Chronicle, 1905

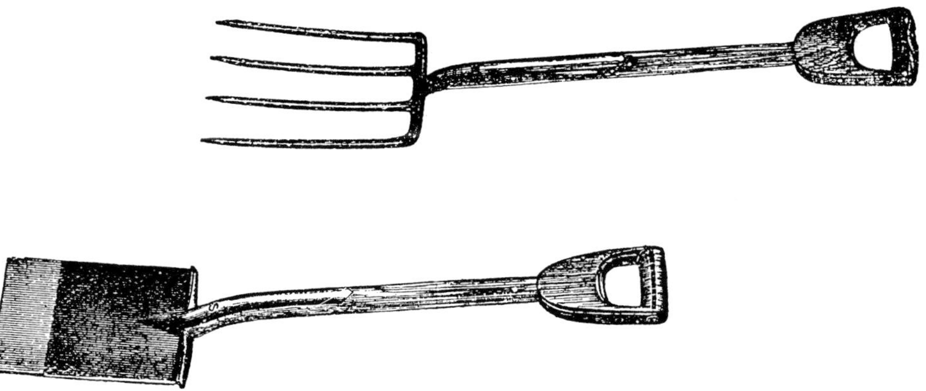

Two Wartime Recipes for Soap

Boil 125g of ivy leaves for five minutes in two litres of water, after which add six litres of water. When cold, wash the clothes in it. It is specially suitable for dark woollens or silk, but is better tepid for ordinary woollens.

The solution is made by shredding six chestnuts upon which is poured four litres of soft water or rainwater. This is left uncovered for four hours. Then filter and warm up. This lathers and cleans like good soapsuds, being specially suitable for stockings, blouses, and fine goods – also floors and kitchen furniture.

Dandelion Leaves as a Vegetable

DANDELION leaves are uncommon even as a salad, and still more uncommon when cooked. They should be washed well and left to soak for an hour. Then blanch them for a few minutes in boiling salted water, take them out and cook them in fresh boiling water. They should take about half an hour. Drain them well, pressing out as much moisture as possible, as with spinach, chop them up finely, and fry them with butter. Add a spoonful or two of cream before serving.

Ambrose Heath, 1941

CLIPPINGS

The Old Mole Catcher

OLD Albert had no qualms about catching those cannibalistic little creatures who could rapidly cover his lawns with hillocks of loose earth, providing attractive seedbeds for weeds and building sites for ants. He would skilfully seek out the run by finding a patch where the ground was hollow; this was usually near a molehill or perhaps between two. The run might be just under the surface or lower down '. . . according to the worm situation. In wet times the worms are at the top part of the ground. In dry weather you're not bothered with the moles so much because they've gone down deeper after the worms. They are still about, but deeper.'

After tracing the run Albert would cut out a piece of turf and put in a trap. Next, he would cover the trap with the turf so not a trace of light could penetrate. He would then wait until a mole came through. Albert set the traps in the evening and would inspect them every morning. Sometimes it could be a whole week before he caught a mole. The moles might also be cunning and fill a trap with earth. The secret was to catch them at the lawn's perimeter before they had a chance to invade the lawn itself, because it is very difficult to repair a lawn and it soon becomes uneven.

Albert once tried poisoning the moles, but he does not favour this method. 'You can use poison, but you've got to get a permit because it's strychnine. You collects the worms in a jar and then you feed them strychnine. Next morning you put the worms in the runs, but its only got to be the deep runs so when the moles have it, nothing else can get at it and pass it on.'

It takes from 300 to 350 moleskins to make a fur coat, and when Albert was a boy he used to collect their skins to make some pocket money. He would cure the skins himself by stretching them on a board, securing them with nails and allowing them to dry. However, Albert found 'It wasn't really worth it. The time they had graded them, you might only have two or three out the dozen that were top grades and you had the price according to the grade.' Nowadays Albert takes pleasure in occasionally helping out in a few local gardens.

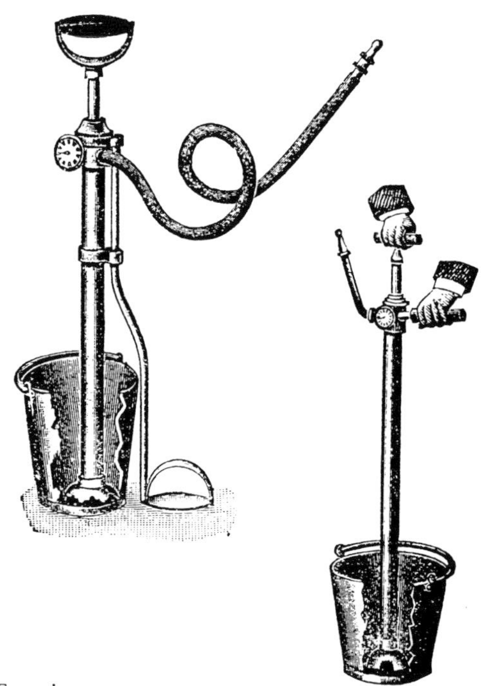

Enemies

MICE . . . Breakback traps we set everywhere, and at first every day had its victim or victims, though later on the little creatures seem to have learned wisdom and avoided toasted cheese and smoked bacon. We found they did not touch bean seeds when they were sown with a little red lead, and for a time the smell of paraffin with which we rubbed the boxes of our frames kept them off, but when it grew fainter with time they came again. Finally we introduced a kitten into the garden, who began to make a havoc among the mice, but the fear of her being trapped in the midst of a gaming country such as ours, led us to feed her lest she should wander, and since then her life has been one of luxurious pauperism.

Helen Nussey and O.J. Cockerell
A French Garden in England, 1909

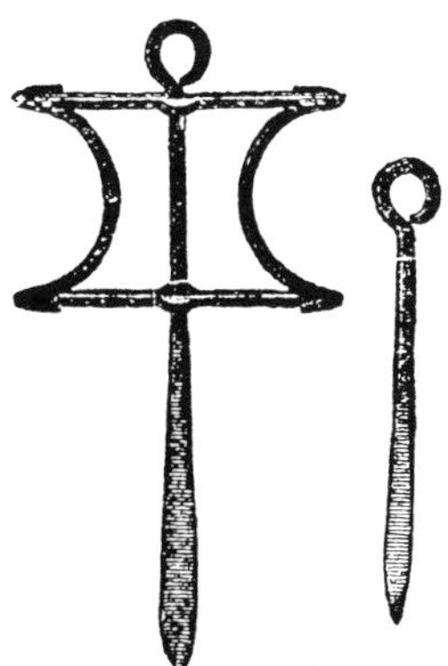

Weeds

TO the layman and the uninitiated in general, the study of weeds may seem a dull and unprofitable occupation; to them weeds are a nuisance and nothing more, but to the good gardener the study of weeds makes many appeals . . . The gardener recognises in weeds foemen worthy of his steel; enemies in the destruction of which all his skill and ingenuity are engaged. By dint of waging ceaseless war upon weeds, the gardener has learned many a useful lesson which in their absence might have remained unlearnt.

Gardeners' Chronicle, 1910

Flags

IF anyone having a few spare eaves to drop had dropped them near our garden fence on a certain day last week, they might have overheard me drawing the attention of Robinson to 'the German, or bearded, type'.

If from that they had deduced that we were Fifth Columnists or deep in a discussion of racial physiognomy, they would have been wrong. To begin with, we weren't deep in any discussion, we were just beginning one. And we certainly weren't concerned with such things as Aryan whiskers. Our talk, at my neighbour's request, was of the Iris.

I had explained that there were many different species. The bulbous rooted Spanish, Dutch and English Irises, which must be planted between August and October; the Japanese sorts, which thrive best in very damp places, such as the edges of ponds; the Cushion and Beardless varieties; and finally the Bearded Irises, comprising the popular May and June flowering plants known to most gardeners as Flags and to others as German Irises, Orrice Root or Fleur de Luce.

'I presume you're really interested in Flags?'

Raymond W.B. Keene, *Over the Garden Fence*, 1946

Garden Gestapo – The Greenfly

DISTINGUISHABLE from the blue-bottle by its absence of steel helmet and stripes, this insect can be found in the garden clinging to lettuces, old bicycle tyres and empty tins. The most destructible of pests, a single greenfly has been known to eat a whole rockery and many of the wretched creatures made their way into Kew without paying for admission. It is an established fact that they breed in the spring mostly without going through the marriage ceremony. Codger says that the best way to deal with the greenfly is to ignore it, but an ounce of stale skate dissolved in drain water and applied to your marrows will teach it a lesson.

Peter Ender *Up the Garden Path*, 1944

Olé

'TWO members of the Women's Land Army, Mable Sales and Joyce Newton, employed by Captain Pryce-Jones, of Frenchies Farm, Mark Cross, a few days ago pluckily drove off a bull which had attacked and gored their employer. Captain Pryce-Jones, who is well-known in the Tunbridge Wells district, was engaged in tying the animal up in its stall when it suddenly turned on him. It knocked him down and commenced to gore him. His shouts for assistance were heard by the girls, who ran into the stall and after driving the bull off, succeeded in rescuing their employer by dragging him to safety.'

The Argus, 1944

CLIPPINGS

The Royals Visit the Allotment

DURING World War II, Geoffrey Sleeman and his brother were billeted in the country to escape the bombing in London. 'During the evacuation, our school was kept separate from that of the country boys and girls, and we had a Nissen hut for our lessons; but we'd got no books or pencils, nothing, because there was a war on. They had to keep us amused somehow, and we'd go out on nature rambles identifying foxgloves and blackberries and so on. And collecting acorns for the farmer so that he could feed his pigs. Then they gave the school an allotment to use, and this became the be-all and end-all of everything.

'When we got to school one day, the headmaster called us all together and said "We are going to have some very important visitors today. I can't tell you who, till they arrive, so I want you all to get your wellingtons on and get working down on the allotment." Who should arrive to see how London children were coping with evacuation, but the King and Queen! They did a tour of the allotment, speaking to some of us (not to me).

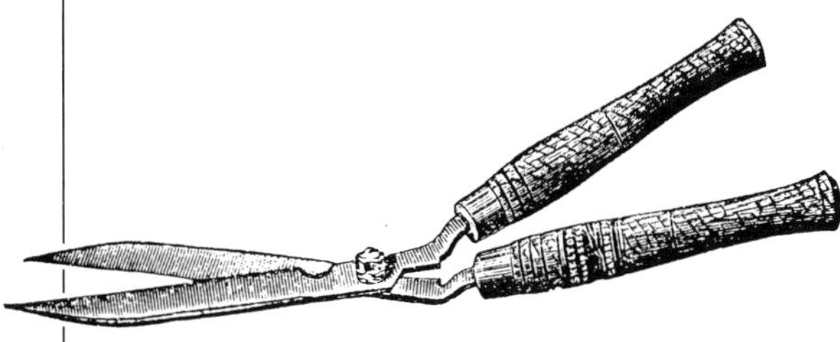

'After they had gone, the headmaster declared a half-holiday. My brother and I walked home (it was about a five-mile walk) chattering excitedly. Of course we were early, and that was the last thing the maids wanted. "What are you doing, playing truant?" "No, guess who's been to visit our school today – the King and Queen!" And they didn't believe us, and we were sent to bed without an evening meal for telling lies!'

The Gardener's Life was a Hard Life

THE garden has seen many changes and today, with the help of mechanical tools, only a few staff are necessary at one country house, Polesden Lacey, Surrey, compared with 38 before World War I, and 14 in 1938. Life for the staff is easier today in more ways than one: at one time there were notices forbidding them to walk upon the lawns; if caught, on the first occasion it cost the culprit a fine of half a crown, with worse to follow, for if disobedient a second time, apparently dismissal was the punishment.

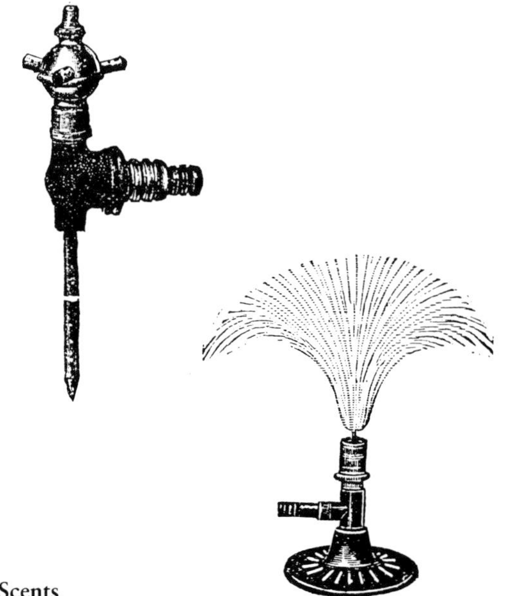

Scents

To-day I think
Only with scents, – scents dead leaves yield,
And bracken, and wild carrot's seed,
And the square mustard field;

Odours that rise
When the spade wounds the root of tree,
Rose, currant, raspberry, or goutweed,
Rhubarb or celery;

The smoke's smell, too,
Flowing from where a bonfire burns
The dead, the waste, the dangerous,
And all to sweetness turns.

It is enough
To smell, to crumble the dark earth,
While the robin sings over again
Sad songs of Autumn mirth.

Edward Thomas, 1918

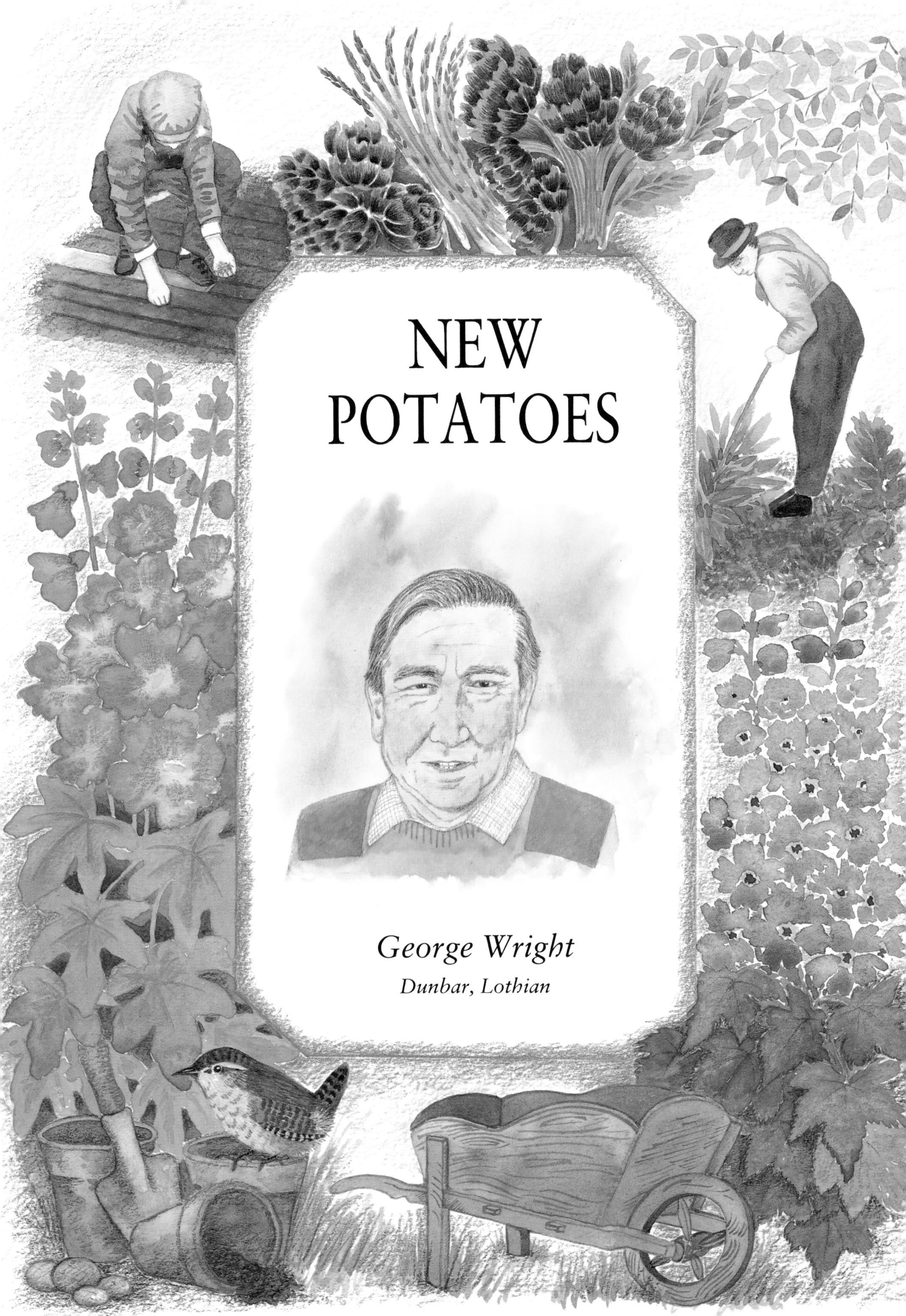

NEW POTATOES

George Wright

Dunbar, Lothian

George was fourteen when he went to see the grieve, or gaffer, on the estate near Dunbar where he lived in the early thirties. Everyone worked on the estate, there was no other work available.

'"I finished school today, is there any chance of a job?" "You'd better go up and see the Colonel." So I went up to the back door and the maid fetched him. He had a cigar in his mouth, blew smoke all over me. "Who are you? What do you want?" Well, he knew who I was, because he had seen me around, thrashing rats at harvest and all that sort of thing. I explained, and he said "When I send for you, that will be the time to give you a job." It was his attitude that got me. I went off, muttering to myself, but an hour later the farm grieve came up and said that I could start work on Monday.'

George gave a hand with the potato harvest which was in progress at the time. They had two hundred and fifty acres of potatoes, dug up in the field and put into baskets. It was a back-breaking job. 'A lot of people used to come from Ireland, from Donegal, I think. They would stay in the bothy, about thirty of them. Some of them used to drink all the money they earned. Three or four would bring their wives with them to do the cooking, but no children. And the fishermen's wives came too, when the fishing was bad. The field was marked out with little sticks and flags. Then the baskets of potatoes were tipped into the carts to be taken to the riddles – a series of sieves; the Potato Marketing Board decided the size of the riddles. Four women checked over the eating ones, called 'ware', to see there were no bad ones, then they

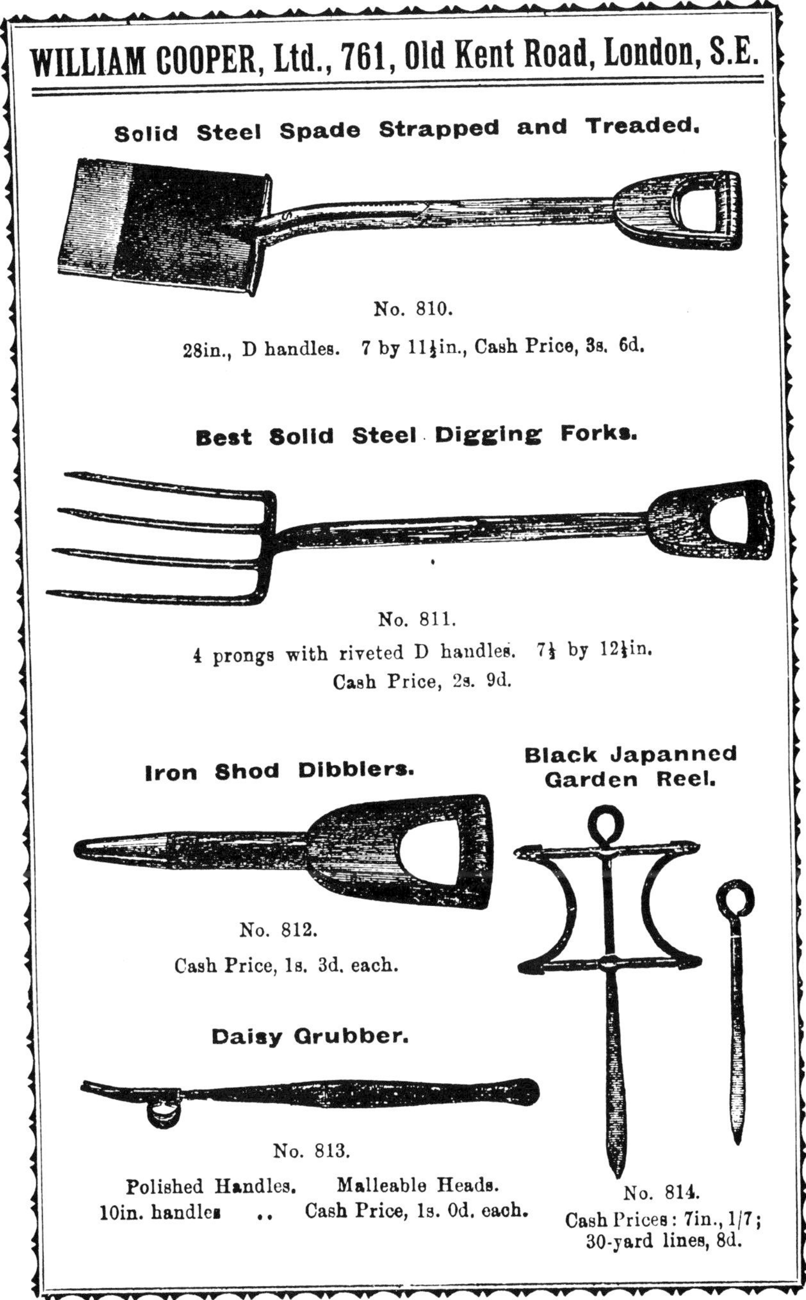

went into the sack. The smaller ones were for seed and came out of a separate spout and went into a separate clamp; the others went for cattle feed. They were called 'brock', which is the Scottish word for rejects – they might have chips on them, or worm-holes. You got 22s 6d a week instead of the usual wage of £1. The men would work the riddler and the elevator, and the women picked them over.'

When the harvest was finished George was promoted to the gardens, which were substantial, with large areas of greenhouses. The farm grew a lot of potatoes and the greenhouses were used to experiment for new strains. To reproduce them, the potatoes were cut into little pieces around the eye and each bit planted with its eye. One good potato might have eight or nine eyes. They were dipped in lime to keep the slugs away, and planted close together to keep the new potatoes small. When they were ready, they went to the farm to be planted out in a field that had not had potatoes in it for five or so years, so there was no chance of the new strain getting mixed up with the old strain.

Potato seed was sown in boxes. 'We might sow half a million seeds and just get one which was a really decent one.' It would take five or six years to get something new. George tended one called Dunbar Standard and another called Dunbar Cavalier, which grew well on the local red soil. He also remembers Doon Star, named after the hill of that name. 'That was an excellent potato, a good seller locally. But it didn't sell too well in England as it was too mealy – most people in England like a watery sort of potato, and this was a very mealy one. It was a good cropper and a nice potato. We'd boil them up with the skins on, and take the skins off after they were cooked. You want a potato which hasn't got very deep eyes, you know, which you've got to get out. We used to get 5cwt of potatoes a year free, that was the perks on the estate. If you didn't want them all, you used to get the money at the end of the season. My brother and mother worked on the estate too, so we could get 15cwt, but we didn't need all that. The most money we got, though, was only 4s 6d – it should have been 3s 9d a hundredweight.'

They used solid fuel for heating the greenhouses; someone would go with a couple of horses and carts and bring the coal straight from the station. They grew grapes, which were rooted outside the greenhouses; peaches which were hand-pollinated by the head gardener, Jock Mackay, with a rabbit's tail on a cane; and cut flowers, for sale to the local hotels which catered for the golfing visitors. If it was too hot they had to whitewash the glass to deflect the sun, then clean it off again later.

The gardens had a huge avenue with trees leading to the house and parkland on each side, protected by a ha-ha. George had to mow the grass with a mower pulled by a horse. 'We had to put rubber things on the horse's feet, so as not to cut the grass up. It was a huge big mower, but it didn't pick the grass up, you had to rake it up. You had to walk to the side otherwise you got covered in grass. We used to use Clydesdales, a heavy horse, but it has a smaller foot compared to the Suffolk Punch and all them. It was quite a performance getting the shoes on them. I used to like mowing. Bess was the horse's name, she used to know exactly what to do, she had done it so often. Otherwise we had to use push-mowers, heavy things, there was no petrol mowers in those days. That was really hard work!'

The climate in this part of Scotland was not too severe. The estate was sheltered by the Lammermuir hills, and there was not much frost with the salt in the air from the sea. They did have cold winds, however. 'I didn't like apple pruning. We used to grow all standard trees then, and that was a cold job, up the ladders. You'd be there all day doing one tree, and you couldn't really see a result. November was a cold month, when we did it. Digging was all by hand, of course. The vegetable garden was walled with sandstone walls, with fruit trees around it, too. We used to buy the reject nets, the old nets, from the fishermen; when they thought the nets were beyond repair they

would get rid of them and, we got them for nothing, more or less, and cut the good pieces out and draped them round to keep out the birds. Hang them down in a bit of a clump, held out with a stick. We used to take the fishermen down a few potatoes, all barter system. Then red lead was used to protect the peas and the beans. It had to be mixed up, and it was a devil of a job to get it off your hands afterwards. And we used washing-up liquid for greenfly – anything that had greenfly on it – using a syringe.'

As well as the garden itself, the farm was about two thousand acres, barley and swedes as well as potatoes. Then there were the oats and corn for the horses, and

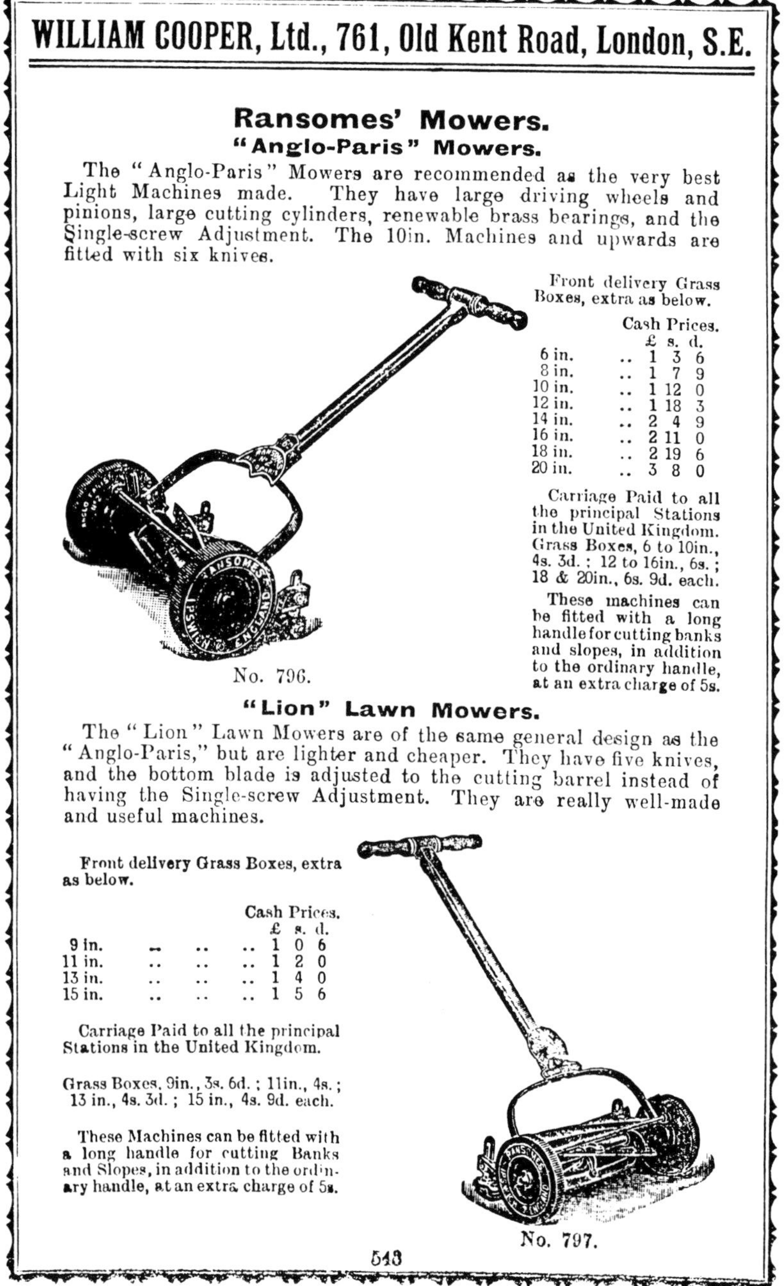

WILLIAM COOPER, Ltd., 761, Old Kent Road, London, S.E.

Ransomes' Mowers.

"Anglo-Paris" Mowers.

The "Anglo-Paris" Mowers are recommended as the very best Light Machines made. They have large driving wheels and pinions, large cutting cylinders, renewable brass bearings, and the Single-screw Adjustment. The 10in. Machines and upwards are fitted with six knives.

Front delivery Grass Boxes, extra as below.

Cash Prices.	£	s.	d.
6 in. ..	1	3	6
8 in. ..	1	7	9
10 in. ..	1	12	0
12 in. ..	1	18	3
14 in. ..	2	4	9
16 in. ..	2	11	0
18 in. ..	2	19	6
20 in. ..	3	8	0

Carriage Paid to all the principal Stations in the United Kingdom. Grass Boxes, 6 to 10in., 4s. 3d. : 12 to 16in., 6s. ; 18 & 20in., 6s. 9d. each.

These machines can be fitted with a long handle for cutting banks and slopes, in addition to the ordinary handle, at an extra charge of 5s.

No. 796.

"Lion" Lawn Mowers.

The "Lion" Lawn Mowers are of the same general design as the "Anglo-Paris," but are lighter and cheaper. They have five knives, and the bottom blade is adjusted to the cutting barrel instead of having the Single-screw Adjustment. They are really well-made and useful machines.

Front delivery Grass Boxes, extra as below.

Cash Prices.	£	s.	d.
9 in.	1	0	6
11 in.	1	2	0
13 in.	1	4	0
15 in.	1	5	6

Carriage Paid to all the principal Stations in the United Kingdom.

Grass Boxes, 9in., 3s. 6d. ; 11in., 4s. ; 13 in., 4s. 3d. ; 15 in., 4s. 9d. each.

These Machines can be fitted with a long handle for cutting Banks and Slopes, in addition to the ordinary handle, at an extra charge of 5s.

No. 797.

543

turnips too. They had thirty-two horses and sixteen men for ploughing: 'A lovely sight, really. And there were two odd horses with young boys to do all the carting about. There were "orra" men, too – the men who didn't drive horses. Then there was the land for forestry. Each year about fifty or sixty acres were cut down and planted again. A lot of wood was used on the estate for fencing work and so on. The estate was well kept. All the gates on the road were painted once a year, with the hinges oiled.

'There were also two shepherds who lived up in the middle of nowhere, in the heather. They couldn't have children, as it was too far from the school. They had perks like a ton of coal a year, and their own cow. If they stayed there for a long time they were not spending much money – after, say, twenty years they could save maybe £500, which was a good deal of money in those days. Then they could get a house nearer civilisation.'

George used to beat for the shoot in the season on a Saturday, for which he received four shillings extra. He hated killing anything, but it was a nice outing. 'I'll tell you what we used to do, unofficially. There were a lot of rabbits there. Sometimes a pheasant would come down when no-one was looking and we'd poke the pheasant down the rabbit hole and put some leaves over it. We used to go back at night with a carbide lamp, an old bicycle lamp, and try to find it. It was a luxury you see, a pheasant. And we had two lakes, one was private, but anyone could use the other, and we used to do a bit of fly fishing. There was quite a lot of trout. A burn came down the glen. The head gamekeeper made his own flies and he would tell me which to use, and give me one. He was clever really, he knew, depending on the conditions. The big nobs would buy all this stuff and get nothing!

'We had no electricity in our cottage, we had paraffin lamps, and a black lead stove for cooking. The cottages all had a big stone outside, mostly slate. Every morning the women used to scrub them, and put a bit of white stuff round the sides of them. You didn't notice it when it was wet, but when it dried it came out white. Everybody had different designs. Hearthstone it was called, you used to buy it from the ironmonger's. The cottages were built of red sandstone, sometimes with white sandstone round the doors. You always used to find a stone which was worn away, where people used to sharpen their knives. The women especially.'

George and the other gardeners took their lunch with them to work. 'We couldn't afford a thermos, so we had a tin flask and an old woolly sock to keep the tea warm. We had a couple of sandwiches rolled in newspaper. I remember one chap who had started with us – he was a bit arrogant, really, and left the paper lying around, under the apple tree. He was told off, but he took no notice and was given the sack for the week. Then he was taken back on again, but it learned him a lesson, you see.

'We were treated as well as any other people really, and we were assured of a job and a house. Of course if you did answer back, they could soon

George Wright with the tools of his trade in 1974

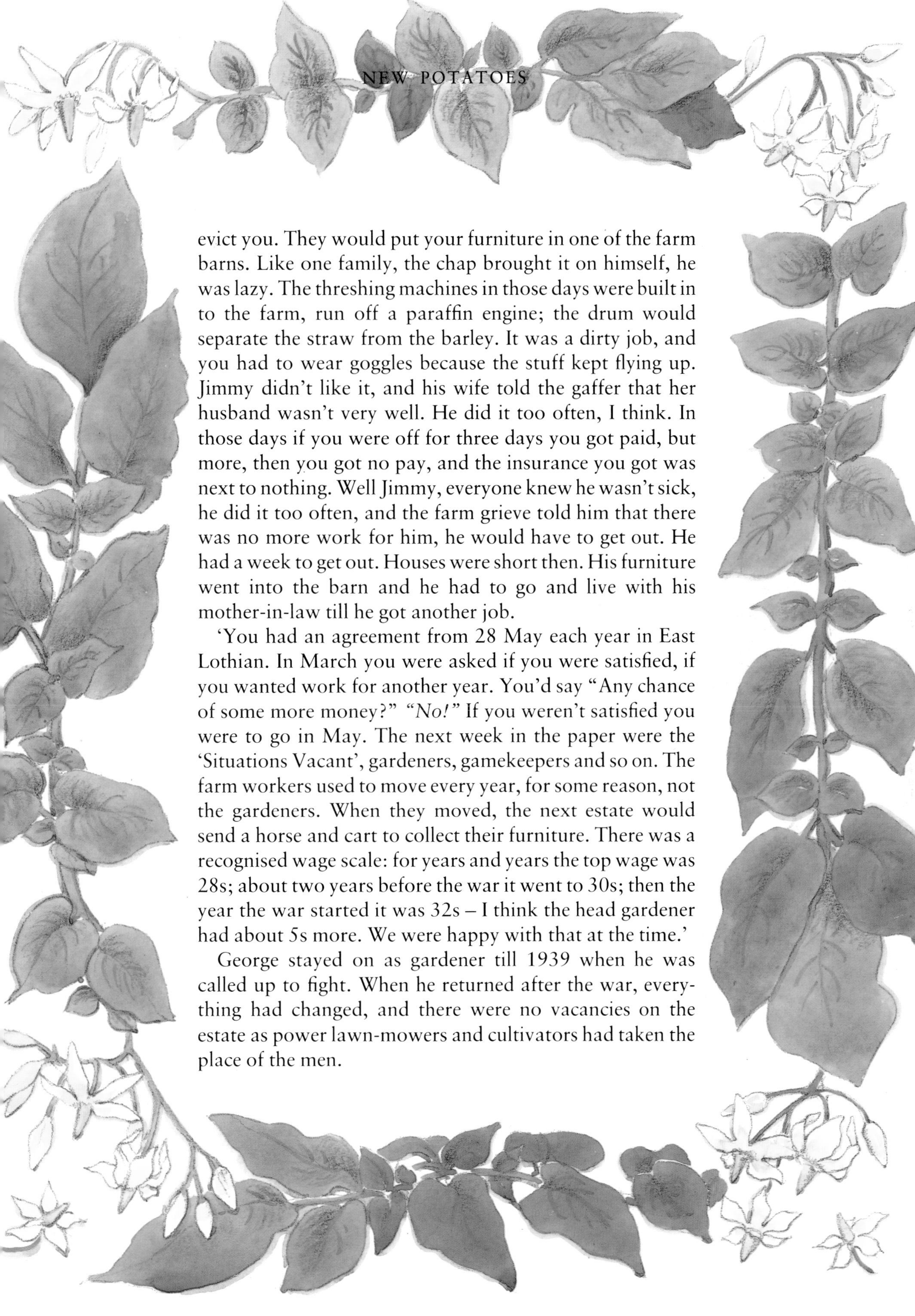

evict you. They would put your furniture in one of the farm barns. Like one family, the chap brought it on himself, he was lazy. The threshing machines in those days were built in to the farm, run off a paraffin engine; the drum would separate the straw from the barley. It was a dirty job, and you had to wear goggles because the stuff kept flying up. Jimmy didn't like it, and his wife told the gaffer that her husband wasn't very well. He did it too often, I think. In those days if you were off for three days you got paid, but more, then you got no pay, and the insurance you got was next to nothing. Well Jimmy, everyone knew he wasn't sick, he did it too often, and the farm grieve told him that there was no more work for him, he would have to get out. He had a week to get out. Houses were short then. His furniture went into the barn and he had to go and live with his mother-in-law till he got another job.

'You had an agreement from 28 May each year in East Lothian. In March you were asked if you were satisfied, if you wanted work for another year. You'd say "Any chance of some more money?" *"No!"* If you weren't satisfied you were to go in May. The next week in the paper were the 'Situations Vacant', gardeners, gamekeepers and so on. The farm workers used to move every year, for some reason, not the gardeners. When they moved, the next estate would send a horse and cart to collect their furniture. There was a recognised wage scale: for years and years the top wage was 28s; about two years before the war it went to 30s; then the year the war started it was 32s – I think the head gardener had about 5s more. We were happy with that at the time.'

George stayed on as gardener till 1939 when he was called up to fight. When he returned after the war, everything had changed, and there were no vacancies on the estate as power lawn-mowers and cultivators had taken the place of the men.

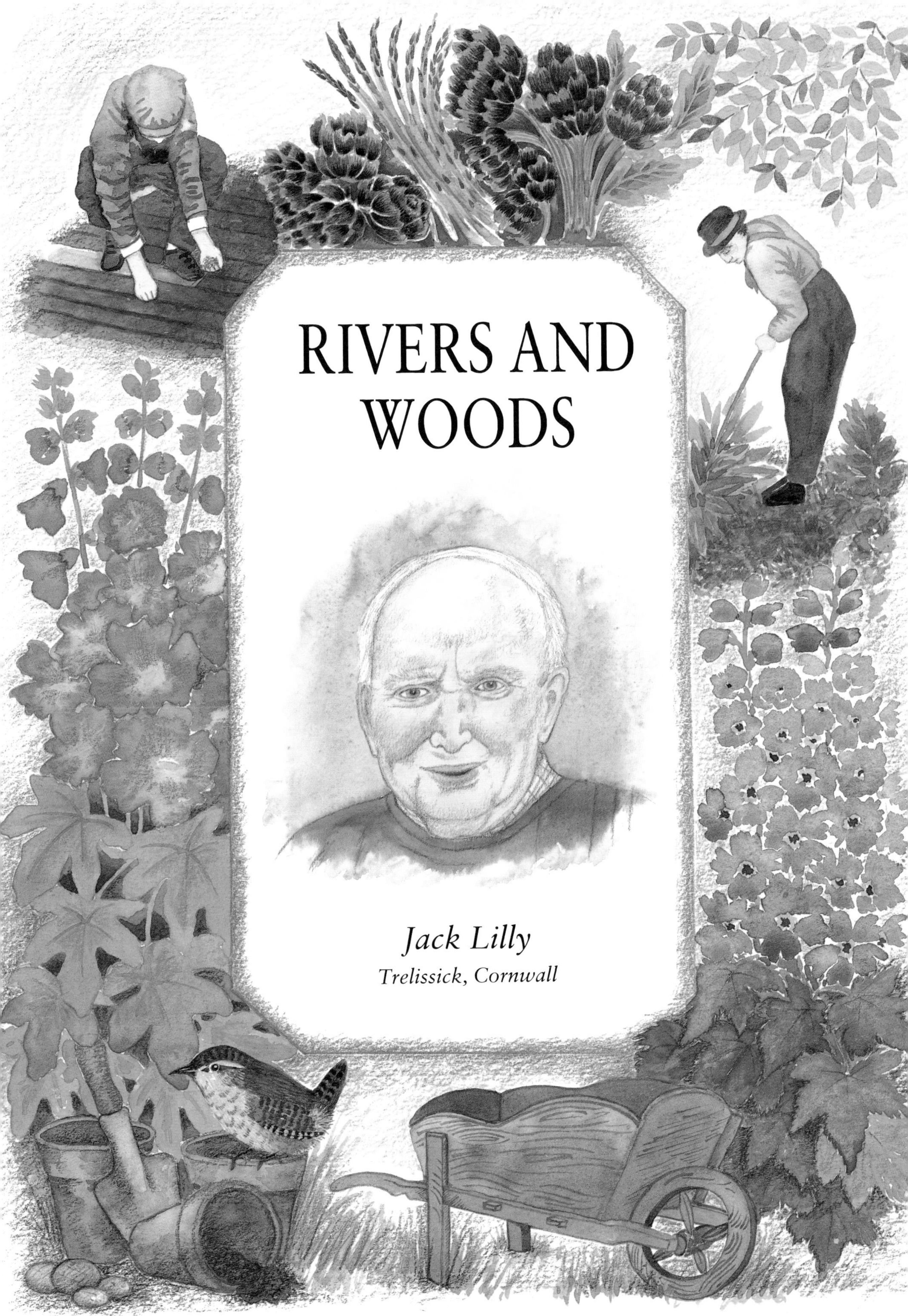

RIVERS AND WOODS

Jack Lilly
Trelissick, Cornwall

When he was young, Jack Lilly climbed a tree in the gardens at Trelissick for a dare. 'I climbed right up the tree, right to the top, then went out onto a branch and swung down one branch after another till I reached the ground safely. Mad, they said I was. I should have been a monkey. I loved doing it.' Jack was born near Trelissick in 1914, and has always worked there or nearby in Cornwall. Although he is not now so agile as he used to be, his small size and quickly smiling face mean that one can imagine him climbing high, whether for a dare, or carrying a saw in the course of his work.

In the early 1800s Trelissick house had 'a large walled garden, well clothed with fruit trees, a good orchard behind the house and a handsome lawn in front'. The Daniell family developed the house and the estate, landscaping the woodland park. In 1821 the family owned nineteen hundred acres and the owner could ride to Truro without leaving his land. Later on the estate became known for its outstanding

orchards, and for its exotic plants. In 1913, L.D. Cunliffe, a governor of the Bank of England, leased and then bought the estate, bequeathing it to his stepdaughter Ida Copeland in 1937. She and her husband are largely responsible for the layout of the gardens we see today, and for the planting of rare shrubs, particularly hydrangeas, magnolias, rhododendrons and camellias. The gardens slope down towards the King Harry Ferry road, which is hidden, and up again on the other side. In 1955 Mrs Copeland gave the gardens and the woodland walk to the National Trust, together with an endowment to help with its maintenance.

WILLIAM COOPER, Ltd., 761, Old Kent Road, London, S.E.

No. 33.

Improved Wall Fruit Protector.

This form of Wall Fruit Protector will be found most convenient, it being easily detached or attached at will. It is also the cheapest form introduced, and it is strongly recommended. The price includes the wall fittings, 21oz. glass, and the necessary lights; painted one coat.

Price: 1s. 7d. per foot run. If less than 25 feet is ordered 1s. 10d. per foot.

Wall Cover.

This Cover is made in sashes in lengths of 10ft. of good sound, well-seasoned deal; the stiles, which are 2in. by 3in., being well mortised and pinned to tenoned rails, properly rabbeted for the glass, and fitted with 2in. sash-bars. Complete with 21oz. glass; and strong cast-iron brackets necessary for fixing same. All woodwork painted one coat. The whole put on rail at our works (being marked in readiness for erection) at the following respective prices:—

No. 34.

Length.	Width.	£ s. d.
10ft.	2ft.	0 18 6
20ft.	2ft.	1 10 0
30ft.	2ft.	2 6 0
40ft.	2ft.	2 15 0
50ft.	2ft.	3 10 0
60ft.	2ft.	4 5 0

Length.	Width.	£ s. d.
10ft.	2ft. 6in.	1 2 0
20ft.	2ft. 6in.	1 16 0
30ft.	2ft. 6in.	2 10 0
40ft.	2ft. 6in.	3 3 0
50ft.	2ft. 6in.	4 5 0
60ft.	2ft. 6in.	5 0 0

From the eaves of the glass coping, tiffany or other protecting materials may be suspended.

One of the first things you see when you approach the gardens today is a stone water-tower. This was used to supply water for the house and gardens, and also for fighting fires in the neighbourhood. The estate staff provided the manpower. A bell was housed in the top of the tower. 'We had to ring the bell, but when you gave the rope a severe twitch, the bell overturned. Then we had to get the keys from the gardener to go up and set it right. You had to walk over a plank on top of this huge tank to get there. And on the way up, there's fifty odd steps on the way up, you passed the apple storage rooms. Very often you'd give it a good twitch to turn the bell over, so you could fill your pockets with apples.'

There is hardly anything left of the kitchen garden now, and the greenhouses have gone. They used to grow fruit such as peaches and vines. 'In the winter, you had to scrape off all the vines' dead bark. These days you would just spray, but in those days you went out into the field and waited for a cow to do its business and then you would water that down and plaster the vine with watery cow-dung and paint it all on the vine. That drew out all the bugs and that, that were in the vine. Then you could wash it all off and get rid of all the bugs. In those days all we had was tar oil, winter wash, something like that. Today you would spray something on and hope to kill it.'

Jack also had to prepare the soil in the cucumber house. 'I would have to go out

WILLIAM COOPER, Ltd., 761, Old Kent Road, London, S.E.

Workmen's or Gardeners' Cottages.

No. C33.

Three-room Cottages, containing Two Bedrooms, each 9ft. by 7ft.; Kitchen, 14ft. by 13ft.; and Scullery, 6ft. by 6ft.; specially suitable for estates, large works, &c. For Specification, see pages 412 and 413.

CASH PRICES.

Delivered to nearest Goods Station within 100 miles, and erected complete on purchaser's foundation, in Blocks of two, as illustration, £60 each, or £116 per Block; six blocks, £110 each; twelve Blocks, £104 each; or marked for re-erection, bundled and put on Rail or Wharf, one Block, £84; six Blocks, £80 each; twelve Blocks, £75 each, if ordered at one time. Brick chimneys not included.

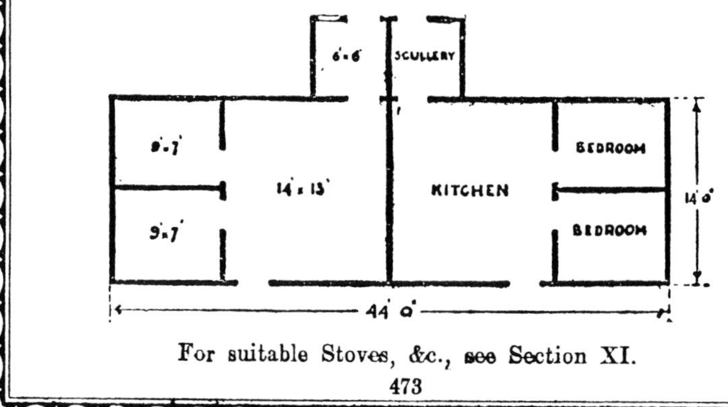

For suitable Stoves, &c., see Section XI.

473

and get all the rotten dung that I could find from the compost heap, and dig it into the bed. Of course there was no such thing as a rotavator in those days. We used to fork everything, not even use a spade as they do now. Then I went into the bed and pulled it apart with my hands, go through it with my hands. Mr Norman, the head gardener, was always there to see that you had done it properly.

'Mr Norman was a lovely character, really. We used to get up to all sorts of things. We used to have four big peach houses. One day Charlie brought out some lovely peaches and stuffed them in his shirt. On the way out though, he met Mr Norman who just looked at Charlie and kept him talking, and talking and talking, and all the time the juice from the peaches was soaking down his shirt. By the time Charlie got back to us, "Well," I said, "look's as if you want a spoon, mate!"'

There is a *Koelreuteria paniculata* growing outside the kitchen garden today. Graham Thomas, gardens advisor to the National Trust, told Jack that if you have one of these in the garden, then you've always got love in the house. 'They used to have the bothy there in the old days and a gas house. At one time they made their own gas for the house. There's a pit there, a round pit made of brick, now filled in of course, which was the gasometer. No one lived in the bothy, at dinner time the boy would go in and make the fire, and if you had a pasty given to you, you could warm it up, sit down at the table and eat it. Later on they made their own electricity in a building beyond the water-tower. They made their own electricity for the batteries they had round the walls of the kitchen garden.'

Jack started at Trelissick in 1931 when he was sixteen, earning 10s a week (having worked for two years at Tresseders Nursery in Truro, where he started at 2s 6d a week). When Jack came, the owner was Mr Cunliffe; after he died, his step-daughter Ida Copeland inherited the property. Her husband's family were the Copelands of Spode-Copeland china, in Stoke-on-Trent. 'Mr Copeland was a great big chap. One day he said, "Come on Jack, we'll go and cut up some of the trees in the park." It was a hot day and his wife appeared with some guests. "You're killing Lilly there." "Go on with your boating, we're quite all right here, aren't we Jack?" Soon as they were out on the boat, "Come on Jack, that'll do" – he didn't want to go boating, you see. He was a grand old chap. He used to wear a top hat when he was going out, and looked very posh. They were grand days.

'It was hard work, it was really hard work. In the winter you get a lot of leaves from the trees here. I was the boy here before the war, and there would be two men raking the leaves and two boys wheeling them away, with a wheelbarrow. Well, a wheelbarrow in them days was a great heavy thing, wooden with an iron band round the wheel in front. And you never just strolled away with the leaves, you ran like the

devil! Nobody told us to, we used to see who could be first. Then you'd turn the load over, and run back again. I suppose it was for the love of it, and the pride.'

Tools were provided for Jack and the other gardeners, all labelled with Mr Copeland's initials burnt into the handles. Some of the equipment which Jack used is on display now. The Dennis lawn-mower, with a 24-inch cut, is a lovely old piece of machinery, dated 1928 and 'built like a tank. One of the real old mowers'. Mr Copeland used to use the Wade cross-cut drag saw, 1920. Jack had to start it, as Mr Copeland couldn't. It was no easy task: 'You lifted it onto a block and the blade would go to and fro. You could wheel it out into the estate and cut a huge old tree with it. Now of course you'd just use a chainsaw.'

There are fewer rhododendrons at Trelissick than there used to be; for example there are no 'Gill's Triumph' or 'Gill's Goliath'. Mr Copeland used to take flowers fresh to the factory so they could be copied and painted on to the china. The rhododendron 'Dot', which was his favourite, is a hybrid between 'Mrs Lindsay Smith' and 'Fortune' and has lovely big flowers. Jack used to grow it from cuttings, as he did so many of the other plants at Trelissick. 'Well, if a gardener can't grow stuff like that, it loses all the interest. Anybody can come and cut grass, or dig a border, but when you can grow something like that, I think it's really nice. When I was with Tresseders at first, I used to have an hour, of course, at lunch-time, and I used to write down all the names that I used to like. I mean back in that little old fernery there I had that fern given me by a chap, *Polystichum setiferum (divisum plumosum erectum lobum)* – it's not that high, but the Latin all means something. I found that if I wrote the name down I could remember it.'

Jack helped to plant the *Pinus radiata* which are now about ninety feet high. In those days, when trees came from the nursery the roots would be loosely balled up in hessian. When Jack planted the *Pinus*, he remembers that Mr Norman dug a huge pit for each tree, put stone and slate in the bottom, and spread the roots out to grow wide from the trunk. They have never blown down. Today, some nurseries grow their trees in round pots; if the tree remains there for a year or more, the roots will curl round in the pot, and they will continue curling round when the tree is planted out and it will flop over unless it is staked for the rest of its life.

'In the old days we used to use a lot of leaf mould for mulch. We also used pigs' manure from the farm over there, and then we would go down the beach and we would cut seaweed from the rocks, mix it with cow-dung, manure and grass cuttings and that, and leaves too; it was turned once or twice a year and was tremendous stuff! We used that for the kitchen garden. Of course for the rhododendrons and azaleas, we used leaf mould for them. Now, as you see, they are trying mushroom compost for mulch, tons and tons of it. I don't know how costly it is.

'The Copelands had two or three houses; one was in Eaton Square in London, another at Juniper Hill in Surrey. We used to pack up the vegetables in great hampers and send them off about once a week. The vegetables for the house here, I used to take them in to the scullery, to see Grace. [Grace became his wife later.] In the old days there was an area of flowers grown specially for picking for the house, and the ladies' maid would come down and pick them. I remember coming in one day, and she had a lovely bunch of rhododendrons. "Where did you get them?" "Oh, I cut them from over there." "What! . . . You did that . . . Next time you can come and ask me, and I'll cut them for you. I don't want you cutting them like that!"'

Jack was still living at home when he first worked at Trelissick, and after a time his mother decided that they were not giving him enough money. Jack approached Mr Norman about getting a rise; Mr Norman saw the agent, and came back to say that he had obtained another shilling a week for Jack. '"Oh, that isn't enough," said my mother, 'cos we had four or five in the family, you see. So I left, and went to work for Tresseders again. But I came back eventually, and the reason I came back, well, I've always loved this place – even when we were at school, at Feock here. Mrs Cunliffe used to invite the whole school to have tea in the house in the big dining-room, and we would play fox-and-hounds in the gardens, hiding in the bushes. I knew the gardens before I came here to work. We used to play down by the crossroads, too. Of course there was no TV then, and no cars, and we would play marbles or football in the middle of the road. I remember my mother going to Truro by a coach drawn by horses. We would go home after school, and then we would go and wait down at the crossroads. About the time she ought to be coming back, we would put our ear down to the ground. We'd say we could hear the horses, though I never could.'

The gales are the worst enemy of the gardens. The Cornish weather is mild and generally frost free, but the wind coming up the wide estuary of the River Fal breaks branches off the trees and damages shrubs. It is said that in the old days a church service would be held on the banks of the Fal by the stone cross on the hillside above the estuary, and the sailors could hear the words from their ships, anchored in the river below, as the voice carried from the cliff to the ships. There used to be steps coming up to the cross from the shore. 'I remember the river here being full up with ships, I remember a dozen ships being laid up because there was no work for them. Now there are about three or four still here. They say they used to use this *Drimys winteri* for the sailors, boil it up to stop the scurvy. It has lovely flowers.

'I brought this *Trachycarpus fortunei* back from Hidcote one time. I used to be a scrounger, but at the same time people could come and scrounge from me. That's what you've got here, either what I've grown myself, or what I've got from other people. This little briar rose, the cuttings came from Nymans and I grew them on. If I saw something good I would try it. Two hundred cuttings is nothing for a propagator. We had mist propagation. We would spend a day making them and putting them in – you took a piece of the plant and cut it off under a node, then you wounded it into the cambium layer and then dipped it into water and into the potting compound. This *Magnolia conspicua* came down in a gale and I took forty or fifty cuttings, and in only eight weeks they were ready for sale. If you took a piece with a bud on, and potted it up, it was ready to come into flower in the shop and that encouraged people to buy it. The *M.* × *soulangiana* is the first one I ever grew from a cutting. It's quite showy, isn't it?

'I planted three different varieties of acers together. I wanted them higher, so I put

an iron stake in them and managed to train them up. I've done very well with the two outside ones, but what happened to the middle one? One day a blasted bird perched there and broke the top off. It's your job to push them up quietly like. They look lovely when they are fully out.'

Knowing the gardens so well, Jack makes an excellent guide. 'See this Japanese cedar, huge tall tree? It had to have its middle cut out, as it tore off in a jagged fashion. I went up with the chainsaw, cut away, and then gave orders to pull the tree over. It wouldn't come. Then it broke, and the brand new chainsaw went over with the tree, and went on ticking over, dug into the ground!' In another case, Jack found that water was collecting in the centre of a huge *ilex* oak, and without action it would clearly have rotted. The ingenious answer was to place a strategic pipe through the tree to drain the water to the ground. Then there is the fig garden. 'I used to go all round there in the branches, from tree to tree, eating as I went – though mind you, I think the birds had more than we did. They are all different varieties of fig.'

Jack became head gardener in 1955, the same year that the National Trust took over. He was responsible for everything outside, including the stables and grooms, everything except the cars. He had four people working under him in the gardens. If he was making up his mind about a young gardener, he would always ask him how he liked the garden. 'You've got to love it. Years ago a young girl came down to work with me for a month. She planted those three Fusiliers over there, and since then she's been several times to have a look and see how they are doing. During the training, they just picked it up from me as we went along. I think they enjoyed their time here, to tell you the truth – they learnt quite a lot, *and* they learnt how to swear!'

Jack's hours were very variable. He would often go out again after his tea, perhaps to cut the grass on a summer's evening. 'The best of it was that my wife would come too, and cut the grass with me. She would bring our little old Mountfield and she'd push it along. She couldn't start an engine herself. She had to fetch me.'

Jack suggested making a ha-ha in front of Trelissick house so that there was no interruption to the lovely view down the Fal estuary. This was done, and it continues for a considerable distance. The only problem has arisen since the public has had access to the grounds, making sure that children do not fall over the edge. There are two summer houses in the grounds; one used to be in a dip and the National Trust wanted to move it higher up so that it would get the sun. They said they needed a crane to do it, as the base was solid granite, but Jack managed the job without the aid of the crane. As for the other one, the rustic summer house, children used to break the glass in its windows so the glass was removed altogether, which is safer but a lot more draughty. Jack laid the entrance to the rustic summer house with boolies (round stones) collected from the nearby Durgan beach.

Another change necessitated by the influx of visitors was the widening of the paths throughout the gardens. Jack liked to encourage disabled visitors to see the magnificent woodland, and used to drive them round in his car; now they have proper electric chairs. Dogs caused an invasion of a different, and not so welcome

Jack Lilly in the porch of his house in 1993

kind, and Jack had to ban them, though they can accompany visitors on the woodland walk. On the other hand, he loves to hear children enjoying the gardens.

At one time Jack used to supplement his salary by growing cacti and succulents. He and his friends would supply the local shops in Falmouth, Penzance, Newquay and Perranporth. He deducted his expenses, took one third and gave two thirds of the profits to the National Trust. In the end they increased his wages, which was better than the uneven earnings he obtained from sales. He has worked hard all his life and is now comfortable on a National Trust pension.

'At one time I think we grew as good a selection of hydrangeas as there was in the country. There's Ayrshire in there, and Joseph Banks. Mr Thomas, every time a new one came out, he would write and say, "Oh Jack, you ought to get so and so!" Of course the following year I would take cuttings, and maybe send them up to Sheffield Park.' (This is the National Trust property at Uckfield in Sussex.)

Unusual trees at Trelissick include the Australian tree fern, the Mexican pine, the snowdrop tree, gingko, tulip tree and the handkerchief tree, and a cotton spruce. The medlar has gone, to be replaced by a hornbeam. 'The *Myrtus luma* is much prized for its red bark. When I cut some down I wasn't allowed to cut it up because the Women's Institute and all that, wanted it for their flower decorations.' Rhododendrons include *R. sinogrande; R. macabeanum* with its huge leaves; *R. arboreum* (red) and the outstanding *R.* Loderi 'King George'.

'In the days of the Copelands we had four big beds of herbaceous plants. One of them would be empty for most of the year, then we put sweet peas in it. We cut sticks, four big clumps about ten foot high. Marvellous, it was – with asters in front of them, 'Ostrich Plume'. It went on for years and years and years. Then that bed was full of crinums. Oh, they are a devil to move – they go down and down and down . . . The Frencham rose has been in the borders for years and years, and these patches of *Primula 'Guinevere'*. Then we changed the beds under the National Trust; I suppose it's better, really.

'They used to have a play here, the National Trust, a stage under the tree and all the audience sat on the lawn. I've seen it full up with people. In latter years they've had it on the paved area by the restaurant. I always used to think they were going to ruin things here. But they didn't, at least not all that much.'

Jack was encouraged by the National Trust to show his plants, and one year he won thirteen first prizes at the Cornwall Garden Show. He would also compete at the shows in London. He has done a lot of judging too, but the driving to shows has got too much for him lately, and he is only doing one this year. Jack is very proud of his British Empire Medal, won in 1978, and he has every right to be proud of his achievements at Trelissick, too.

NOTE: We learnt with sadness that Jack Lilly passed away in January 1994.

THEY WERE GOOD TIMES

Dennis Lindup

Clwyd, Bedfordshire and Warwickshire

'As a boy I used to buy tuppenny packets of seeds from the local shop and grow flowers to take to the market. I used to get 6d [2½p] a bunch for them, or something like that, for pocket money and did quite well, so I decided to go in for gardening; but it wasn't easy in those days.' Dennis Lindup, the son of a blacksmith, was born on the 16 December 1916, at Sweeney Mountain, three miles from Oswestry, in Shropshire. It was difficult to find gardening work: 'Chaps going into gardening always reckoned on getting into glasswork first if they could. Anyway, when I was fourteen, my father got me into Brogyntyn Hall. He had met the head gardener a few times, and there came a vacancy, and I got it.'

Dennis was fortunate enough to have a bicycle and would set off every morning on his four-mile ride. 'I had to be there before seven in the morning so that I could fetch milk for the bothy and the head gardener and be back by eight o'clock. There were four in the bothy and I had to cook the breakfast, and I had half-an-hour for that. Bacon and eggs was mostly what they had. I had about an hour to wash up, then I had to go down to the Hall to see the cook, to see what vegetables she wanted. I had about an hour for that, especially if there were celery and leeks to dig up and savoys to be cut. Potatoes came in in the winter and there was a place to keep those. In the early part of the winter there were grapes and apples and I took them down to the housemaids. Then I would come back and wash flowerpots or crocks or something for a short time, and sweep up the greenhouse. I always found a job to do.'

The bothy was a comfortable house, with one room and a kitchen downstairs, and four bedrooms upstairs. At the back was a range of greenhouses, the potting shed and a couple of other sheds. 'They used to have a woman come in, the second keeper's wife, to cook some dinner and I would have to wash up after that, too. There were always things to do. I would tie carnations sometimes. Then about half-past four I used to get some sticks and coal for the head gardener and do any other things that wanted doing. At half-past five we left off in them days, and I would bike home. The girls in the house had to be in by nine o'clock, so it was no good coming back to see them! Anyway I got caught once. The kitchen maid went down to where the keeper's wife did the bothy and after that I brought her home. That started the romance off and I saw her every day for about three years. She left, and of course I left; she went to Cheshire and I went to Chirk Castle. It was all done more or less by letter, and after that she became my wife.'

One day the head gardener at Brogyntyn had told Dennis there was a job going at Chirk Castle, Denbighshire, and had asked if he would like to try for it. 'He gave me a note. It wasn't a long way away, about seven miles. So I went there and found Mr Jones, he was the head gardener. He said "I've had thirty-two letters, and I've had a lot of callers. I can't make any promises." So that was that.' About a week later, however, Dennis was told that he had got the job, so off he went to work at Chirk under Mr Jones.

'I had only been there about three months and there was an apple fight going on. Yes, four o' them, and he caught 'em, one pinching the apples out of the fruit room, the other picking them off the trees. Then the one had the sack you see, so they advertised; but they only got two replies and one of them was a student. Mr Jones didn't think much of students.' It was unusual to advertise for new staff – they were more frequently found by recommendation. If an estate was known to advertise a lot it would get a poor reputation; workmen would become suspicious of the conditions offered and it would be considered not worthwhile to seek employment there.

'In some places it was by word of mouth, but then of course there was the old man who went round selling pictures, "Picture Jack" they called him. He used to come round and he'd have his dinner in the bothies and then he'd move on. Of course, he'd have a natter with the head gardener and get a pound or something off him. The foreman and the head gardener, they got a lot of information of these places, off this old boy, what was good and what wasn't good. He wouldn't get much for his pictures, so I don't know how he did for lodgings or where he slept at nights. He used to go all over the country, they reckoned, but he'd call and he used to have his dinner. And he'd know what time to come!'

After the lad had been given the sack for apple fighting, Dennis was put on two months' trial working in the greenhouse, and felt himself very fortunate to be able to keep the job when the trial period was over. He continued to work in the greenhouses and with the fruit and carnations, and he used to go to the house in the morning to help with the flower arranging. 'A couple of times I did the dining-table on my own!' Dennis laughed heartily. 'The first time, I decided to do the table with pyrethrums, but I'd not seen the dining-table before,' and Dennis remembered being amazed. 'It was set for eight, and I'd got four vases to do, and there was a great big gold cup and how many knives and forks and glasses, I don't know. And there was me, with the pyrethrums dripping water all over. I'll get murdered, I thought.' Dennis could hardly tell the story for laughter. 'The rain had tumbled down with a thunderstorm just as I was getting near the Castle. Anyway, nothing was said and I got away with it.

'I had some fun at Chirk Castle. We used to go out on the lake at about eleven o'clock on a Saturday night when it was moonlight. There was another lad out of the bothy, the keeper's son George, and me, one would have the canoe and two the rowing boat, and we used to race across the lake half the night. Well, there was a place out there where you'd hit the ground, it was a sandbank or something, and the thing was to avoid it. Some say it was where the river came in, but I don't know. The river might have been the boundary, because the pub in Chirk itself was closed on Sunday, but the one at the bottom of the bank was open on Sunday. The servants were only allowed to go to dances in Chirk.' Traditionally, public houses in Wales always closed on Sundays, whereas in England they opened.

After Dennis had been at Chirk for a year and nine months the foreman recommended that he, along with three others, should move on to Woburn Abbey, in Bedfordshire. He was very surprised when he had a chauffeur to meet him on his arrival at Woburn Sands, and remembers the head gardener was a gentleman. 'We worked under a foreman; they had forty-five gardeners working there.' He found his experience of working under glass invaluable, and got on very well there working in their great range of greenhouses.

The bothy comprised accommodation over the cart sheds and was not particularly cosy. They had a woman to cook for them, though they cooked their own breakfast. 'We paid our bill for our food, dividing it out between five of us. When Christmas came round we were given 7s 6d. At Chirk Castle we were given 3lb of meat each, and the girls got a pair of black stockings.'

Unfortunately, Dennis's time at Woburn was interrupted when he had to go into the Royal Air Force, but the wage of 14s a week that he earned whilst serving his country was made up by the Duke of Bedford to the sum of 35s, the agricultural wage he had earned at Woburn. Dennis thought the Bedfords generous and was impressed that Whipsnade Zoo was given to the nation by the Bedford family.

Sadly, Dennis's most vivid memory of Woburn is of when he was leaving to go off to war, and it is not a good one: 'A chap did himself in while I was there, who'd been there forty years. I went in the bothy and there were four of them there, one or two had been in France, in the Great War, and they were having their meal. They started teasing me and made out I would be in the ground and started singing "When the poppies bloom again, When we go marching over you'll know it's us you hear". Well, he got up and went out. There was a well at the back with a slab on it – all the time I'd been there it had never been altered. Well, I got up, too, and went out to see the head gardener; he always came out at two o'clock after he had had his dinner. He asked if a taxi at half-past five would be alright, and said that George would take me round the garden as he had to go somewhere. Well, we passed the well and George commented "Some lads have been playing here". We went further round and someone asked "Have you seen Harry?" Then again, two or three time, like. Then someone saw his hat and cigarette were floating on the water. They put a stone on a

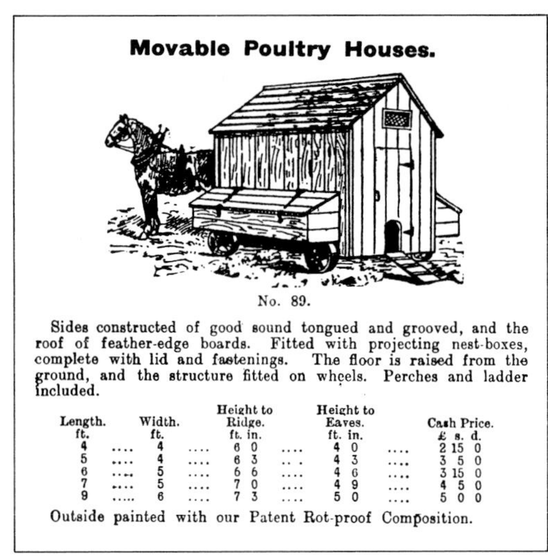

Movable Poultry Houses.

No. 89.

Sides constructed of good sound tongued and grooved, and the roof of feather-edge boards. Fitted with projecting nest-boxes, complete with lid and fastenings. The floor is raised from the ground, and the structure fitted on wheels. Perches and ladder included.

Length. ft.	Width. ft.	Height to Ridge. ft. in.	Height to Eaves. ft. in.	Cash Price. £ s. d.
4	4	6 0	4 0	2 15 0
5	4	6 3	4 3	3 5 0
6	5	6 6	4 6	3 15 0
7	5	7 0	4 9	4 5 0
9	6	7 3	5 0	5 0 0

Outside painted with our Patent Rot-proof Composition.

line and it was about twenty-five feet deep. So they sent for the fire-brigade, but I'd left before it came because it was half-past five. The bombs had upset him, and when they started on me it had upset him again.'

Dennis decided not to go back to Woburn because he was anxious to get a position in the neighbourhood of Craven Arms where his wife's people lived. He had about eight weeks' 'de-mob leave' in which to look for a new job, and seeing an advertisement in the *Gardeners' Chronicle* for a gardener wanted at Packwood House, decided to put in an application. He was given an appointment to meet the head gardener, Mr Weaver, who took him to meet the owner, Mr Baron Ash. 'Ash and Lacey had made their money in the Great War on barbed wire, millions of miles of it. Before that they made cow troughs from corrugated and sheet iron.' Mr Ash and Dennis got along well together and Dennis got the job; then he plucked up courage and asked if he would be able to keep some chickens. Mr Ash replied that was a fair question, and gave Dennis permission to use the spinney. Dennis and his wife were delighted when he got the job: 'We went to two sales in the same day! We'd got the house, but had no furniture.'

The poultry were a great help to Dennis and his wife because food was still rationed. It did not cost much to feed the chickens because in the harvest fields there was often loose corn around under the trees where the machinery could not reach. Dennis soon got to know the farmers, too – and some of the local authorities: 'One day I was on my bike and I'd got some crushed maize and I was stopped by a

Packwood House. In the foreground are the famous yews which represent the Sermon on the Mount (Birmingham Post & Mail)

policeman. He pulled up on his motorbike and said "What have you got in that bag?" "I've got some maize," I said, and rattled it, like. "Where have you come from?" "Packwood House," I told him. "Well, I might as well kill two birds with one stone. Does anyone go fishing in that lake? Do you think I'd get permission?" "Well, you might get a chance if you ask, but it's not up to me, kind of thing." So off I went, and he didn't bother me no more. When the local bloke came, he said someone had been pinching coke at Hockley Heath.

'The local policeman used to come in for a smoke and a chat. I learnt my driving with him, going around houses at night looking to see if there were any burglars about.' Perhaps it is in the nature of policemen to kill two birds with one stone?

Packwood House is renowned for its yew trees, but they were not without problems and developed a 'scale' disease. Some men came from Pershore College to look at them and it was decided that it was due to bad drainage; but Dennis thought they had been over-sprayed, or perhaps the chemical was too strong. New drains were installed some three feet deep – but then it became necessary to water in summer. Fortunately there was a pump to bring water up from the lake. 'And it's all very well to be a conservationist, but if a brook isn't cleared out it will get full of sedges and a field will not drain properly.'

The yew garden was laid out by John Fetherston between 1600 and 1670 and is said to symbolise the Sermon on the Mount, with fat yews and thin yews, tall yews and short yews to represent the multitude. The one in the corner was an old beauty, and the old gardener always called it Bessy Braddock after the Liverpool MP. 'She was awkward to cut and we had to put ladders at angles to get over her.'

Clipping of the yews commenced on the same Monday in late summer in each year, and it took seven men fifteen days. Eventually an outside firm was called in, 'but these blokes didn't work in wet weather so it might take three weeks, and it took something like £1,800.'

Dennis remembered the yews being cut at Chirk Castle, but he had had no special training. He says, 'The gardeners learned from each other, and we did it all by eye. When clipping some yews we had to go up forty-two rungs of the ladder – the highest yew was about thirty feet.'

Dennis tried all sorts of ways to cut the yews, and even experimented with a fork-lift truck, 'but you had to have someone to move it and you couldn't get to some places on the terraces. With a ladder one man can work alone.' When cutting by hand they would cut as far as they could reach and then move the ladder round the tree; they started at the top and worked their way down, and would then work from a shorter ladder or a pair of steps. Eventually Dennis devised a satisfactory method of clipping the yews using ropes and garden forks: 'We tied the ropes three parts up the ladder to keep it in place, and then tied them to forks stuck into the ground so they wouldn't slip. When cutting at height you had to be careful holding your shears, not to go in with their weight. Nowadays of course it's all done by electric cutters.' String was used to hold the yews in shape, as wire might cut into the wood, and if these strings broke, Dennis would sometimes have to get up inside the trees to re-tie them.

'On one occasion someone came down to take photographs of us clipping the yews, for an advertising brochure, and they brought a new green baize apron along for me to wear. I wore it for the pictures, but it was away again afterwards. Never mind, the gardeners did get two new shirts each.'

Dennis finds it a most satisfying job to cut the yews: 'They look beautiful in spring with the fresh shoots'; then he went on to joke about a lady visitor he had heard remark: 'They must look dreadful in winter when they have shed all their leaves!' The visitors were often amused by the peacocks. 'By the door there was a foot-scraper, and there was a mirror on the wall and people thought it was to see if their boots were clean before going into the house, but in fact it was for the peacocks – when a peacock saw itself in the mirror, up would go his tail.'

Packwood is also renowned for its Carolean Garden. The cost of the 4,000 tulip bulbs needed for planting it up in the early 1960s was £80, and they had to be taken up each year – as their quality deteriorated they were transferred to other, less conspicuous places. 'We would do this job on nice days in early autumn, and it took three men a day to plant the bulbs. They would drop a line and make marks for the holes evenly along it, then drop them in.'

Dennis grew a lot of herbaceous plants. 'I changed the borders every two years. Two years bedding out and two years herbaceous. No design, just put the lupins and tall delphiniums and dahlias at the back, anthusia and daisies, then polyanthus in front for springtime. When we planted it up we used to put a lot of pea sticks in the

border. We used to cut them just below the plant, then put them in the borders before the herbaceous came up and let the plants grow through. I'd seen it done at Chirk. It looked a sight at first, but they were good support for the plants.'

Dennis is the first to admit he has had a couple of disasters. 'I got caught by an early summer frost one year and lost 810 dahlias. I was up that night at ten o'clock talking to an old gardener and we decided it was OK, but when I woke up in the morning at half-past five, I looked out of the window and everything was white, even the hosepipe was frozen. The grass was burnt where I trod, and you could see it for five or six weeks after. I'd got some cuttings, and I had to find some other stuff to put in, but I didn't have the blocks of colour and it spoilt the effect. After the war, everybody got cameras and it didn't matter what was in the garden as long as it was colourful.'

Some disasters were not of Dennis's own making. There were the squirrels that stripped the sycamore trees of their bark, and there was the Hunt, when perhaps as many as a hundred horses might have gone galloping through, chasing foxes and trampling all over the daffodils. Least forgivable of the vandals were those who stole ornaments from the gardens. There was an old seat that was taken away in the night and found at Sothebys, and a statue that was moved off a bed and taken across the park. This was discovered by the footprints left in the dew. 'Now Packwood is locked up like a fortress. You can't get in there now, it even became difficult to get into our own cottages. There are spy holes and all sorts of things.'

The winter was a busy time. Early on there would be leaves everywhere, particularly from the huge beech; so heavy were their boughs that they weighed down to the ground, and had rooted themselves. Leaves would be swept up in the morning before they had a chance to blow all over the place.

If there were three or four damp, foggy days the men would spend time slug catching. 'It takes some to fill a four-inch pot. We would put in bran and camphor and they would go for the bran. We'd put rows and rows across the garden and catch thousands of them.' In 1993 Dennis caught six hundred slugs by this method in the little garden of his own home.

Pea sticks were collected in winter, and when the weather was really bleak, time was spent washing pots ready for potting up chrysanthemum cuttings and young carnations. In early spring the box would come out of the frames ready for planting along the edge of the herbaceous borders a little later. The gravel paths might need attention, too, because if children had kicked them about the camber would probably have been lost and they would need rolling. 'Once they had an old-fashioned roller with shafts and a pony to pull it and the protective shoes were still there in the house.' [When Dennis left.] These shoes were made of leather and fitted over the pony's hooves; they were also once used to protect the lawn when the ponies pulled the lawn-mowers. During the Great War, anti-gas boots made of rubber were issued for horses, to be worn in the event of an enemy gas attack.

Later in the year the lawns took a lot of mowing and they tried to mow them in a day. 'We had a Dennis, now they have a sit-and-ride. In the war we had a hand-mower because there was a shortage of fuel and a shortage of labour. They had blokes come up from a local home and they would mow all day for ten Woodbines [cigarettes]; one would push and one would pull. We even had some geese to help keep it short! Later on we did get a drop of petrol for the Dennis.'

(Above) Cutting the grass early this century. The ponies wore leather shoes when walking on the lawn to prevent hoof marks
(Opposite) Dennis in the Carolean Garden at Packwood House (Birmingham Post & Mail)

Labour too, became something of a problem. 'There was a girl and a gardener when I first went and there were three of us for twenty years, but when one retired he wasn't replaced, so veg was cut out and they did without flowers in the house, and I put in beech or laurel and gourds.'

In earlier times Packwood House had been very proud of the decorations inside the house, and Dennis was a founder member of the Solihull Flower Club. They would sometimes hold their exhibitions at Packwood House. 'They might have three or four thousand visitors on a Sunday afternoon to see a flower show. We had a flower room and at one meeting we had a draw with no end of good prizes, so I said to Henry, "We'll have a do in that Henry, we'll have ten tickets each!" They were 1s a ticket. We came back into the flower room and one lady said to another in a haughty voice, "I've sold 2,000, how many have you sold?" Well, there was us, we'd spent ten bob. We laughed and laughed.

'As the club got bigger they went to Chelsea and won this, that and the other, and they fell out. They had learnt a bit you see, and they all went off and started separate clubs in their own villages. I'd helped quite a bit, this way and that, and the lady president asked "Is there anything you want?" and I said, "We could do with some new greenhouses." And that's how the new greenhouse came about and I don't think the National Trust know about it to this day!'

The National Trust took over in 1941. 'We weren't told. None of us. The head gardener heard it given out on the news! He said to the housekeeper, "They've given us away, they have. Lock, stock and barrel, to the National Trust".'

Dennis had been happy working for Mr Ash who had treated him very well, and after the Trust took over completely, Dennis would still get letters from Mr Ash. 'He regularly sent me £100 to go on holiday and at Christmas, and sometimes it would be £150. When he was seventy-five years old he sent £350.' Dennis is very grateful because he feels he may not have had the house he has now if it hadn't been for this money that he and his wife saved. 'The National Trust treated me well, too. They left me alone and I was allowed to buy what I wanted, but there was nothing outrageous. I didn't cost them nothing. I gave them more than they gave me.

'Every three years the Trust had a trip, and one year we went to Ireland, another to Sheffield Park and we went to Wisley and the Chelsea Flower Show. There was a trip to Powis Castle and another to Nantwich. Then we met all the other head gardeners and Graham Thomas, the National Trust's garden advisor, would take us round. Sometimes they gave us a book of the place and another time we had to buy them. We had lectures in the evening, but some of them rushed off to the pub. I knocked around with

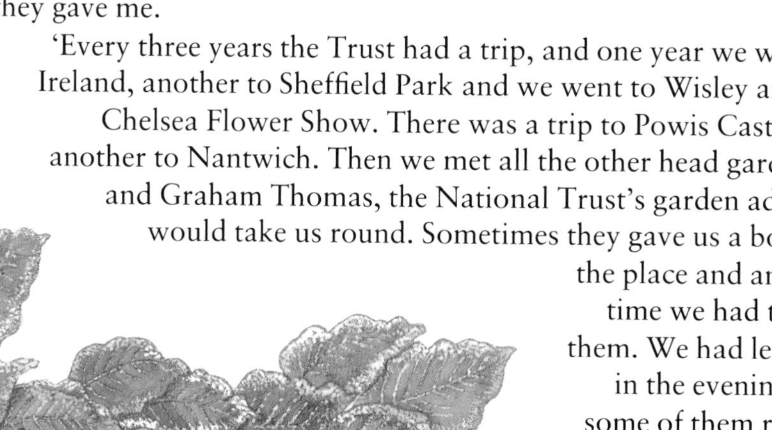

them from Cornwall and we had some fun with the head gardener from Trelissick, Jack Lilly. Once we stopped at The Feathers, in Ludlow, and we wanted bed and breakfast and it was £22.10s. Jack called out "Who's the boss that owns this place? Fetch him here! It would be cheaper to buy it!"'

They were good times, Dennis recalls. 'I had a party when I retired and they presented me with a silver salver, and I got the British Empire medal. So now I'm enjoying myself and keeping busy helping neighbours and friends. I've cut cypresses, beech hedges and yew, and I have my allotment. I go visiting gardens, and last year I went on a trip to Holland to the bulb fields with a lady friend and we had a lovely time looking at all those colours.'

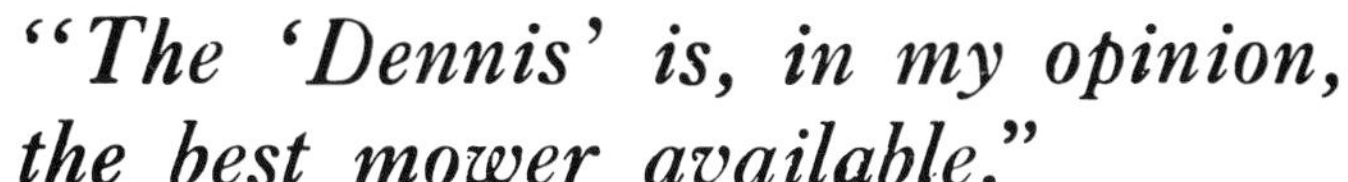

Says Mr. Reginald Beale, F.L.S. (Messrs. James Carter and Co.), in his book "Lawns for Sports."

THE SUPERIORITY OF THE

DENNIS

MOTOR LAWN MOWER

IS RECOGNISED BY THE LONDON COUNTY COUNCIL AND MANY OTHER PUBLIC BODIES AFTER SEVERE TESTS AGAINST OTHER MAKES.

Highly efficient, it stands in a class by itself, and embodies all those characteristics that for the past 28 years have gone to make the name 'Dennis' a household word in the Motor Manufacturing Industry.

So simple is it in construction and operation, that any gardener can work it without previous mechanical experience.

The 4 h.p. engine is powerful enough to draw trailer and driver up steep gradients, and can travel up to 5 miles per hour on the level.

Brief Specification.
4-h.p. 4-stroke engine which is easier to start, much more silent, and can be run at a slower speed than the usual 2-stroke engine, and is fitted with differential gear, which enables it to turn in its own ground; separate clutches for roller and cutting cylinders, so that the machine can be used as a roller only if desired; patent automatic lubrication, detachable covers to driving chains, mechanical adjustment for cutter blades, and many other unique features.

PRICE: Delivered to any Railway Station in Great Britain—
24"—£75 30"—£90
Trailer Seat **£7 : 10 : 0.**
Less 5% for cash within 7 days.

Write to Dept. "G.D." for Illustrated Catalogue.

DENNIS BROS. LTD., GUILDFORD

Manufacturers of the Dennis Motor Lorries and Patent Turbine Fire Engines.

Humming in the Air

THERE is a natural occurrence to be met with upon the highest part of our down in hot summer days, which always amuses me much, without giving me any satisfaction with respect to the cause of it; and that is a loud audible humming of bees in the air, though not one insect is to be seen. This sound is to be heard distinctly the whole common through, from the Moneydells, to Mr. White's avenue gate. Any person would suppose that a large swarm of bees was in motion, and playing about over his head. This noise was heard last week, on June 28th.

Gilbert White (d. 1793),
The Natural History of Selborne

No. 971.

Fancy That

Vicar: 'It's marvellous what God can do in a garden with a gardener's help.'
Gardener: 'Yes, but he makes a hell of a mess of it if he's left to himself.'

A Pruning Tip

ONE of Gordon Miller's favourite jobs was pruning fruit trees. 'My governor asked me, would I go and prune his brother's apple and pear trees? His brother had a son the same age as me. It seemed rather strange that I should go and do his pruning and his nephew was coming to do the pruning on our orchard. They had the old theory there, that you should never prune your own trees, you always asked someone else (who was competent of course), because you might be tempted not to prune them sufficiently severely. If you are doing your own trees, you are always tempted to leave bits in, that really ought to come out. This applies to ornamental things like roses too.'

The Nursery Gardener

ON the edge of the city [Norwich] we met an old nursery gardener well known to my companion. He was the true old-fashioned dissenting type, cropped whiskers, shaven chin and a mouth that turned down at each end, black suit and dicky, a wooden look that suddenly twinkled, a passion for imparting information. I knew that either he would utter the least possible number of words, or if we found favour in his sight, would immediately impart some information to us and instruct us. We found favour. He began to tell us how to grow roses, and as he, like a superb conjuror, knows the trick of bringing up the most extravagantly lovely roses out of the sullen ground, we listened to him with respect.

J.B. Priestley, 1934

Pembroke College Gardens, Cambridge

PEMBROKE College was founded in 1347 by Mary, wife of the Earl of Pembroke. Many notable people have attended the college over the centuries, including Nicholas Ridley, who was elected a Fellow in 1534 and later became Master. He was a distinguished Protestant Reformer, becoming Bishop of London in 1550. He had great influence in the church while Edward VI reigned, assisting Archbishop Cranmer with the Protestant reforms. On the king's death however, he supported the cause of Lady Jane Grey, and after her downfall, when Mary came to the throne, Ridley was arrested for heresy. He was burnt at the stake with Cranmer and a third Reformer, Latimer in 1555. Ridley remembered Pembroke College with much affection, particularly the orchard, 'the sweet smell thereof I trust I shall carry with me into heaven'. There is still a path in the gardens today known as Ridley's Walk. The gardens provide a series of calm and lovely courts for the use of both the college and the public.

On fine days croquet may be played and the Fellows can also play a version of crown bowls. The green is very different from the straight and level lines of the ordinary bowling green. It has a hump in the middle of the turf, and sloping banks around it, all of which are used in play. The grass must be kept fine and close, well fertilised, watered and trimmed. Regular crown bowls is a competitive game played by all ages, men and women, particularly in the north of England, though variations of the game can be found all over Great Britain. It has been known and played for hundreds of years, although the current rules were only formulated about eighty years ago. The exact configuration of the hump and sloping sides of the green is not specified. As in lawn bowls, the competitors must try to get their bowls as close as possible to the jack.

At one time at Pembroke, a large square of this hallowed turf was removed to create a safe place for the burning of a boat when the college went 'Head of the River'. Cambridge and Oxford universities both have events called 'bumps', which are inter-college rowing races. At Cambridge, colleges may enter several boats of eight oarsmen each, resulting in about nine leagues with, say, twenty eights in each league. Girls have their own separate divisions.

The River Cam is narrow, and the boats line up one behind the other. There is a muzzle-loading canon to signal the start. The course is over about two miles and the aim is to catch the boat in front. If this 'bump' is achieved, then both boats stop rowing and pull in to the side of the river to allow the others to pass. Crashes can be spectacular. If the oarsmen in the following boat do not stop rowing immediately they have bumped the boat in front, then the front boat may be driven right on to dry land among the spectators. Or else, three boats may be involved in a crash.

To celebrate the end of the races, each college has a 'bumps supper'. In addition, the winning college, which has gone to the 'Head of the River', will burn a boat. Originally it would probably have been the winning boat itself, but in view of the current astronomical cost of the eights boats, the college will procure an old one of any description, and burn that. In recent memory, when Pembroke went 'Head of the River' they were forbidden to remove the turf from the bowling green for the burning ceremony. Instead the boat was burnt on the drive, no doubt with as much jubilation and high spirits as before.

Gordon Miller went to Pembroke College in the 1960s, and made a big impact on the gardens by introducing new plants and making suggestions for improvements. Lavenders and yews give one court a formal appearance, while another is characterised by a variety of graceful trees. One area is designed to give winter interest, while buildings in another place provide shelter for less hardy shrubs.

Eventually, Nicholas Firman came to work as Gordon's assistant. Part of the training which Gordon instilled into the youngster was never to destroy a plant if he didn't know what it was – it might be worth keeping. One day he sent Nicholas off to clear out some tubs ready for new planting. Nicholas left one of them untouched, and when Gordon came to find out why, he realised what must have happened. A student must have thrown his date stones into the tub, and they had taken root. There were six lovely little date palms flourishing in the tub!

The Flower

Once in a golden hour
I cast to earth a seed.
Up there came a flower
The people said, a weed.

To and fro they went
Thro' my garden-bower,
And muttering discontent
Cursed me and my flower.

Then it grew so tall
It wore a crown of light,
But thieves from o'er the wall
Stole the seed by night.

Sow'd it far and wide
By every town and tower
Till all the people cried
'Splendid is the flower.'

Read my little fable:
He that runs may read
Most can raise the flowers now
For all have got the seed.

And some are pretty enough,
And some are poor indeed;
And now again the people
Call it but a weed.

Alfred Lord Tennyson, 1809–92

Griffinia blumenavia.

Florists

FLORISTS are divided into two kinds: The first is the market-florist, who grows and forces flowers for the market; and of this sub-species there are two varieties, those who grow only hardy flowers to be cut as nosegays, and those who deal chiefly in exotics or greenhouse plants to be sold in pots. The other sub-species is the select florist, who confines himself to the culture of bulbous-rooted and other select or florists' flowers, who has annual flower-shows, and who disposes of the plants, bulbs, tubers, or seeds.

John Loudon, *Encyclopedia of Gardening*, 1822

The First Flower Shows

WHEN the Huguenots first came to England, because of their great interest in plants they brought many specimens with them and formed florist societies. These were clubs where they could meet to exchange plants and discuss horticultural topics. The first florist society met in Norwich and by 1667 there was one in London. They are thought to have been jovial affairs with an annual floral feast where members would enjoy a good midday dinner and then exhibit their flowers in competition for prizes. Although the vogue spread throughout the British Isles and lasted for over a century they were eventually abandoned and replaced by the flower shows we enjoy to-day.

Floral Decoration

'DURING the following years many and much larger decorations took place, amongst which may be instanced what at the time was called hanging gardens of Babylon, on the occasion of a ball given by the Marquis of Bristol, when six tons of cut Ivy alone was used, to give a castellated effect to the bare walls of an improvised ball-room. A few days afterwards one gentleman gave a magnificent entertainment, the flowers for which cost over £500. Various other similarly decorated entertainments followed, the result being that more than £3,000 was paid to one single firm for floral decorations only, in less than one month, and Messrs Veitch, Turner, Paul, Bull, Lane and many other great plant-growers were very largely drawn upon, nothing being considered too expensive or too rare. Magnificent Orchids, Roses by the ten thousand in a single day, as well as innumerable Ferns and other decorative plants were used.'

Journal of the Royal Horticultural Society, 1893

The Tonic

'PARINGS and raspings of horses' hoofs which can be purchased (from the village blacksmith) for very little, put into a tub of water and allowed to decompose, make a very excellent and nourishing liquid manure. It should not be applied too strong.'

Mrs C.W. Earle, 1896

Food for the Soul

LET him who hath two loaves, sell one and buy flower of narcissus, for bread is but food for the body, whereas narcissus is food for the soul.

Mohammed

The Litany

THAT it may please thee to give and to preserve to our use the kindly fruits of the earth, so as in due time we may enjoy them. We beseech thee to hear us Good Lord.

The Book of Common Prayer

Beautiful Gardens

WHOEVER begins a garden ought, in the first place and above all, to consider the soil, upon which the tastes not only of his fruits but of his legumes, and even herbs and salads will wholly depend. And the default of soil is without remedy: . . .

In every garden four things are necessary to be provided for: flowers, fruit, shade and water; and whoever lays out a garden without all these, must not pretend to any perfection; it ought to lie to the best parts of the house, or to those of the master's commonest use, so as to be but like one of the rooms out of which you step into another . . .

The rest that belongs to this subject must be to the gardener's part, upon whose skill, diligence and care the beauty of the grounds and excellence of the fruits will much depend . . .

So that for all things out of a garden, either of salads or fruits, a poor man will eat better, that has one of his own, than a rich man that has none. And this is all I think of necessary and useful to be known upon this subject.

Sir William Temple, 1628–99

CLIPPINGS

Hard Work

JOHN and Maureen Lloyd make their living from their market garden at The Scarr, Newent. Maureen had been a nanny at Sudeley Castle before her marriage, and the caravan which was their first home together was very different. Maureen was unaccustomed to cutting lettuce, which was very boring and very hard work. Her husband slaved for eighteen hours a day, and she for fourteen, or as long as she could. When the children came along, she was extra busy. Now she has got used to the work, and both she and John enjoy getting up at 4am on a summer's morning. Their land has wonderful views of the Malverns, the Cotswolds and the Welsh hills, and these make a beautiful backdrop to the rows and rows of lettuce waiting for attention.

'You either like the job or not. If you worried about the returns, you wouldn't be in it. In my mind, I will always make a living and Mo [Maureen] is the same. We are satisfied with the way of life. You have to make the

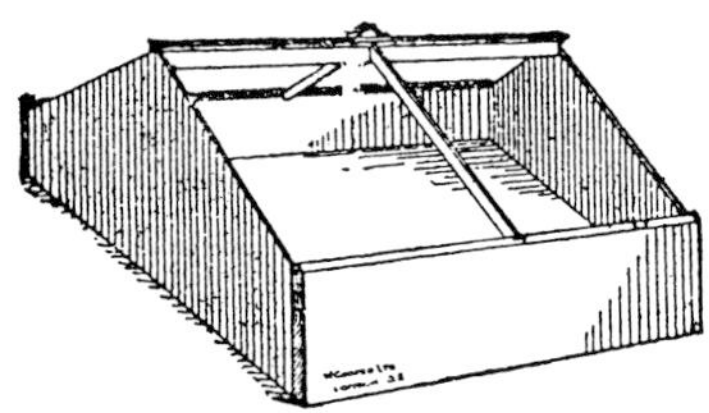

people who work with you enjoy it too, because it is a tedious job. Mostly they do the planting and we do the cutting. When we are making a profit as owners, we are going to feel happy, but it is different for them. You have to joke with them, cheer them up, send them home early.'

John Lloyd believes in running a 'very tight ship' on his four or five acres. He uses old-fashioned methods in his market garden compared with some others in the neighbourhood. He spends nothing on computerised technology control and artificial growing methods, everything is grown in soil, though unlike the olden days, this is not now enriched with manure. Then, manure was collected from the large cities, where the horse and cart was the main means of transport, and it was taken by the load to the market garden areas to be dug into the soil. Nowadays, nutrients which are suitable for each individual crop are introduced to a specific area, and anything extra would be wasteful.

Before planting, the soil has to be broken up thoroughly, whether out in the open or under cover. 'Once, someone was sitting on the small tractor and it went the wrong way. Straight back into the side of the polytunnel. They were wrapped in the polythene till it was stretched to its limit, and then there was an almighty "pop" as it burst!'

From May to July the Lloyds plant celery every week, for cutting in the autumn; celery is a bog plant, and loves the steamy warmth which can be created in the polytunnels. On one occasion John had a certain order for two thousand sticks of celery which he had to pack himself for a particular supermarket; then they phoned to say they didn't want the order. There was no redress – the celery had to be taken out of the special bags and a sale sought elsewhere.

Other crops have been tried over the years, such as leeks. 'We wanted something of an income during the winter. It's one acre, and gives us more work to do during the winter. If you have money coming in, rather than constantly going out, well, you're happy aren't you? Try them wrapped in bacon with a cheese sauce. Lovely . . .'

Maureen thought of growing chillies for the Birmingham market one year, which they did, very successfully. But twenty boxes flooded the market, and that was that. They have also tried peppers and other crops, but John feels that too many growers jump from one thing to another; it only takes 3 or 4 per cent extra to flood the market, whereas a deficit of 5 per cent means profit for the lucky grower. The supermarkets and the wholesalers have the power, and when they whistle, the grower jumps. They don't need the grower, the grower needs them.

'I reckon our life goes in five year cycles. In that time we have one good year, one pretty good, and one bad. We made a lot of money at the beginning of 1993 because with the warm spring there was a high demand for lettuce – so, time to change the car!'

It has been said 'Heaven sent the gardener and the Devil sent the cook to spoil his work.'

CLIPPINGS

Green Tomato Jam

WASH four pounds of tomatoes, take out the stalks and cut out any discoloured part and weigh them. Put them into a colander, plunge this into boiling water, leave it there for three minutes and then drain well. Now slice the tomatoes, and put the slices into a basin, in layers, with three pounds of preserving sugar. Add the juice of lemons and the lemon rind, yellow part only, which you have put through a mincing machine. Cover the basin and leave it all night. Next day strain off the liquid, bring it to the boil and boil it for a quarter of an hour. Skim it, add the tomatoes and lemon and cook until the jam is clear and will set.

Ambrose Heath, 1941

Wildman and his Bees

IN 1772, the celebrated Daniel Wildman exhibited here [Prospect House, Pentonville Road, Islington] his bees every evening (wet evenings excepted). He made several new and amazing experiments; he rode standing upright, one foot on the saddle, and the other on the horse's neck, with a curious *mask of bees* on his head and face. He also rode standing upright on the saddle with his bridle in his mouth, and by firing a pistol, made one part of the bees march over a table and the other part swarm in the air and return to the proper hive again. Wildman's performances of the 'Bees on Horseback' were also described:

He with uncommon art and matchless skill
Commands those insects, who obey his will;
With bees others cruel means employ,
They take the honey and the bees destroy;
Wildman humanely, with ingenious ease,
He takes the honey, but preserves the bees.

John Timbs, *English Eccentrics*, 1866

A Curious Aid to Formal Gardening

WE have received from Dr. Landmann of Berlin, specimens of a curious invention for the purpose of assisting amateurs and others to easily form geometrical designs in their flower beds or window boxes. The aid offered by the inventor consists of sheets of tissue paper, on which the various designs are marked by rows of Cress seeds which are stuck to the paper with an adhesive liquid. In the case of a large symmetrical design it is recommended that the sheet of paper should be spread over the bed and a little fine soil sprinkled over the paper to keep it in place. In the course of a few days the Cress seeds grow and mark out the line the planter is to follow. Having planted his bed, the Cress may be pulled up. The invention is certainly ingenious, but it comes at a time when geometrical flower gardening in this country is probably at its lowest.

Gardeners' Chronicle, 1910

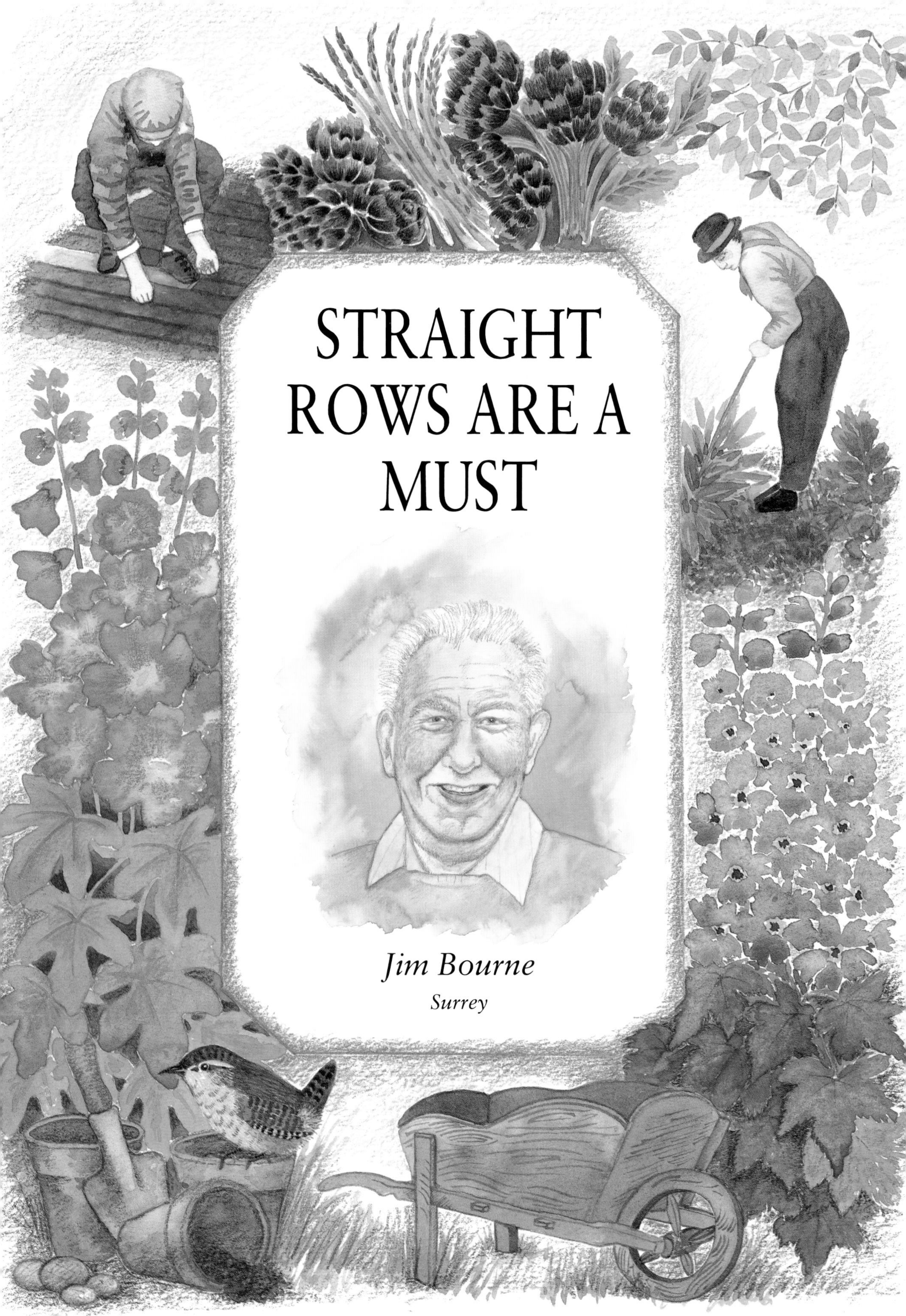

STRAIGHT ROWS ARE A MUST

Jim Bourne
Surrey

Interrupted only by a spell in the Royal Air Force whilst on National Service, Jim Bourne followed a gardening career all his working life. Born in June 1927 in the little village of Ashurst Wood, between Forest Row and East Grinstead in Surrey, Jim started work at the age of fourteen as an under-gardener to Mr Albert King at Combe Place, East Grinstead, where he stayed for four years.

Jim believes it was at Combe Place that 'the groundwork' was laid that was to stand him in good stead for the rest of his gardening life. As each job came along and Jim went to various estates, he always complemented his knowledge learned in the garden with study in the evenings. When he was studying for the Royal Horticultural Society senior exam he worked eight-and-a-half hours a day, and then studied from about half-past six until ten o'clock for five nights a week. It was hard, but Jim acknowledges that this was the best way to learn about the techniques of gardening. He also found the help of Mr King invaluable, particularly for plant identification. 'As we walked in the garden on our way to various jobs, he used to give me three plants a day to remember. He would give me the proper name, the Latin name, and the common name if I wanted to know that. If we walked that way again three weeks later, he would say "What's that?" and I was expected to know it! Well, you get three plants a day, and we used to work five-and-half days a week, that's eighteen plants a week, fifty-one weeks a year. We only had one week's holiday. On four years, you multiply that, plus the ones you wanted to learn yourself anyway, for your studies, it works out to be a lot of plants!'

Jim later became a pleasure-ground foreman, and then at twenty-eight years old he was appointed head gardener to Major Broughton at Bakeham House, Englefield Green; he continued as such to Sir Michael Sobell who later took over the estate. Eventually Jim moved on, and spent the next sixteen years working on the Cranleigh estate until, sadly, he was made redundant. However, as the saying goes: 'One door closes and another door opens' – and it was at this point that Jim reached what was perhaps in many ways the most rewarding part of his career.

Jim became instructor on the Springbok estate at Alfold, Cranleigh, in Surrey. This was an institution originally founded by the people of South Africa and their government in recognition of services given to them by Great Britain during the war. It was then funded by the National Union of Seamen and the Manpower Services Commission. Springbok was not only a training establishment but a convalescent and retirement home as well, with ten bungalows for retired seamen. The men Jim was involved with at Springbok were mainly ex-seamen who, because of illness or injury, were unable to go back to sea. They were given a choice of doing one year's training in poultry work, farming, or in horticulture and Jim proudly recalls that during the fifteen years he spent there, of 240 people, 180 went into horticulture. 'Some are still in the industry and hold jobs at various well-known nurseries and estates like the Royal Gardens at Windsor and the National Trust.'

The one-year training course covered the whole spectrum of gardening, including fruit and vegetable growing, cut flowers, pot plants, salad crops and care of amenity areas. The men were taught to use all kinds of machinery if their disabilities allowed this: there were strimmers, hedge trimmers, a range of mowers, cylinders and rotary

Jim Bourne on the Springbok Estate stand at Cranleigh Show

cutters, both petrol and electric; three types of mechanical rotavator; tractors, a mini-tractor, an ordinary tractor with a plough that could hitch on behind that, and a four-foot rotavator could go on behind the tractor, too. There were also shredders, mixers, chainsaws and bench saws.

The year's course took the men to the City and Guilds Phases 1 and 2 qualifications, and they were also able to take examinations and proficiency tests with the Agricultural Training Board according to their aims and abilities. At the end of their training every help was offered to find them jobs. Some of the men were suffering from nervous disorders, and working on the land offered quietness and an easy-going routine which, in contrast to the hubbub and noise of the winches and wheels on a ship's deck, was of immense therapeutic value.

There were, of course, many problems, as the trainees included alcoholics, schizophrenics and epileptics, and Jim found that although he was teaching horticulture, there were a lot of underlying things to be considered when dealing with the disabled. 'Your mind is at it seven days a week, preparing for the next day during the evening and over the weekend for the following week.' It was necessary for Jim and his colleagues to attend a range of courses, to help them cope with any difficult situations that might arise, and Jim often found his own solutions to help the men cope with their various disabilities. 'With alcoholics it was difficult for them to admit their problem, but once they *had* admitted it the battle was half won. Schizophrenics

take patience; to make them want to learn they had to be motivated and kept interested – once they became bored there were troubles. My solution was to give them more to learn than they knew they could cope with. To keep them busy; to really keep them busy.'

Jim was obviously very sympathetic towards the men he taught, and pointed out that for the alcoholics the only thing to do was to reduce the chances of their getting a drink, but with his jolly nature he cannot resist a chuckle over some of the pranks they got up to. 'The places you found bottles was really quite funny, in leaf-mould heaps, even manure heaps; under frames; hidden everywhere. The funniest one of all that I found was a bottle tied on a string and on to a piece of wood and gutter, hanging down a stack pipe! I knew the chap had one somewhere, because he was really smashed out of his mind, but it took me over an hour to find it!

'Once an alcoholic, always an alcoholic, but to help them we had to be aware of their plight and reduce the chances of them indulging. Once they had realised their situation, what they did was to take counselling courses from us.' Jim has one splendid success story to tell. 'Two men took counselling from us while attending day-release courses. They are not cured, but they are safe now and one has become a full-blown counsellor himself, counselling alcoholics. I think it's a lovely circle. He's helping the ones who are in the same trouble as he was.'

There were also epileptics, and they were not allowed to use machinery as this was forbidden by the Safety at Work Act, but Jim finds it gratifying that epilepsy is so much more easily controlled nowadays. Defective eyesight also meant special care with machinery; consequently, the number of trainees on a machinery course was sometimes limited to as few as thirty per cent of the trainees. The rules were strictly followed, because one accident, and the establishment would have been closed down immediately. 'The Health and Safety Executive are very severe, but they need to be. They do things in a sensible way.'

There were those with physical disabilities, too. Several men had only one eye, some had suffered badly broken limbs, and there were those with low mobility for other reasons. Jim admires the way some of the men coped with their physical disabilities, and particularly remembers a man with only one hand. 'His hand was off just below the right wrist. He learned to write with his left hand, and to prepare cuttings he managed to hold a razor blade between the claws of his right hand. He prepared cuttings like ninepence, and did them faster than anyone with two hands. The razor blade would flash in all directions!'

Following a change around, the Health and Safety Executive regulations became even more severe so that not only were instructors required to be proficient at all the skills they also had to gain teaching certificates, so they too had to attend classes.

'That was a novel experience, I can tell you. I had about two years to go before I retired, and I had to go back to school! We had to learn how to handle chemicals and spraying. I didn't have to have a certificate to use the apparatus and chemicals, that came under what they called "grandfather's rights", that is, age exempted you and they accepted you knew enough about it to be safe anyway. What it was, was that you had to have a certificate to be able to *teach*. Classes were held at the local agricultural college for about four days. It was rather funny, really. There were about twelve of us there from all sorts of jobs; when we first met, each of us was given a name tag and we had to introduce ourselves and say how long we had been using chemicals. The men were standing and they went round the room: "Well, I've been in the job six months." "I haven't used chemicals at all." "I don't know anything about spraying." "I've been in the job two years and I have six months chemical experience." Then it came round to the chap who was on the course with me. "I've been on the job in agriculture for twenty-two years." Old Dave and I used all sorts of spraying equipment, including boom sprays behind tractors, high pressure stuff for the last sixteen years. He looked at me and said "It's your turn now," and I said, "No, I don't think I will!"' Jim chuckled. 'Well, I've been in the trade just on fifty years and I've been using chemicals and spraying equipment for forty-eight – and I'm still on this damn course!'

All gardeners have their fads and fancies and Jim admits he is a stickler for *straight rows*. 'Straight rows are a must for me, and have been since I first started gardening, or even a bit before this as well; there must have been a seed there of some sort before that, my father being a gardener. His father was a gardener too, and I had three brothers who were gardeners and one worked on a farm, so we were in allied trades, so to speak. My first lesson in straight rows was when, together with the head gardener I was with, I got the ground ready for this onion bed during the winter months. We prepared in the normal way as we did for onion beds in those days,

Straight rows are a must for Jim!

digging about two feet deep and letting the weather get at it through the winter, and then applying all the soots and wood ashes in the spring. We worked the seedbed down and then came the time for sowing the onion seed. He got the tools out of the shed and took me down to the kitchen garden to show me what to do. He put the line down and drew out one drill: it was absolutely gun-barrel straight. "There you are, I want thirteen more drills like this. Exactly the same." I drew them out the way he had told me to and then gave him a shout and he came down. He looked at it and said, "Well, you can rake the whole lot in and draw them out again, only this time get them straight and get them all the same depth because the depth varies as well as the straightness." I drew them drills out in the finish *fourteen times* before I could satisfy him, and all the praise I got at the end of it was "Why the devil couldn't you do that in the first place?" Since then, I have had a thing about straight rows myself! I realise now that he was an exceptionally good teacher, he really was. There's no such thing as a *nearly* straight row, it's either straight, or it isn't.

'If you think about it, anyone that walks down a vegetable garden should get as much pleasure out of seeing vegetables growing as they do flower borders and rose beds. I think they should look just as nice. In some circumstances, especially in private service, an employer demands that; it is one of the things he will look for. He gets just as much pleasure from all parts of the garden as one part.

'Straight rows are only for the person doing the growing. The vegetables don't give a damn – they don't care if they are in a straight row or a crooked one! I've done runner-bean wigwams in herbaceous borders for years, and have had people pick the flowers and put them on dining-tables! They got shot for it, but they did it!'

When Jim's turn came to instruct, over forty years later, he too was a hard taskmaster as far as straight rows were concerned. 'I was instructing on putting up some runner-bean rows. They were long rows, 85 yards long. I was called away to go out for the best part of the day and I left a staff man there who knew what I was like about straight rows; and when I returned I saw that instead of putting the canes along the line as they should have done, each stick they had put in had pressed up against the line, pulling it slightly out each time so the row had finished up nearly four foot out of true! It was like a crescent, a new moon. The time was getting on, it was late in the afternoon, and they had not only stuck it, they had railed and tied most of it too. But it was so offensive to my eye, I said, "That's it. Cut the strings, pull the sticks out and stick it again!" I wasn't very popular about that, one or two slight criticisms, to put it mildly.'

Jim explained that bean rows can be erected in a variety of styles, but Jim favours the Sussex style. 'For the Sussex style the rows are usually stuck about 18 to 24 inches apart and the sticks are crossed about half-way up. Next, a parallel rail is put in on the top of the 'V' and one round underneath on the inverted 'V', and they

are tied securely. You put in fresh hazel benders and you put them in vertically and bend them over and lock them down underneath the rail and tie them, not only on the cross-rail, but on each of the sticks that they cross. No gale will ever move it. I have had bean rows in even an autumn gale when the plants have been full of foliage and beans, when the beans have been completely stripped but the sticks have still stood! Another style, as opposed to my sort of fashion, is to tie them very high up. They cross the sticks about a foot from the top and if you get that tied and locked, that's tight. They usually use only one cross-rail.

'When I've stuck a row of runner beans, I maintain you can get a pair of steps and walk along the valley, and you should be able to see through the whole length of the row. You cross the sticks, put the cross-tail through the top and tie on alternate sticks as you go along. You stick your knee up under to get it really tight, so that it really jams it, and then you can tie the sticks on the underside on the alternate ones opposite to the top; in that way each pair of sticks is tied. I will only use hazel because it stays warm; it's better than ash, because for some strange reason ash stays cool. Beans will grow faster on warm hazel sticks than on cold ash.

'For pea sticks I prefer good flat hazel, fan-shaped hazel, cut fairly early in the winter, or the sap in the hazel will throw the leaf and make it look untidy. Largest sticks go in along the row first. If you've got a four-foot garden pea, you use a five-foot stick and go along and trim the tops with secateurs so that it looks nice and neat like a hedge. The sticks you take off the top you stick down the bottom in between the big sticks, so that it starts the pea off and you don't waste anything.'

Jim enjoyed his life at Springbok, and particularly remembers the part they played in the Cranleigh Horticultural Show. 'I was persuaded to put up an exhibit, not knowing at the time it was a competitive thing. I thought it was just an exhibit from the estate to let people know who we were and what we were, and what we were trying to do here; and lo and behold we won the first prize and the cup the first year! Well, I decided that we had to go in for it again the following year, and we won it again the second year! "The best horticultural stand." There was a terrific amount of stuff; I think we took two vanloads of stuff and a horsebox full, because we were selling it all, of course. What we did, we had the spare stuff stored underneath the tables, and as the people bought it, we replaced it, so the exhibit looked as good all day long, as it had at the time we were judged. So, what happened? We were getting our legs pulled like mad. "That was a fluke, that was! That was dead lucky, you daren't go in for it a third time!" Well, with that, we had to, and we got the cup again! Three years on the trot, that was a hell of a morale booster. We were over the moon, and it was good for the estate since each man had had a hand in growing the produce, you see. It was good for the trainees as they were all involved. No one single person took all the limelight.'

Springbok achieved this success using up-to-date methods – modern chemicals and fertilisers and so on – and Jim talks about trendy organic gardening with some reservations. 'I remember that when I first started gardening, that was practically all it was, organic. Now, there are so many people talking about organic gardening and jumping on the organic bandwagon; even up to a certain royal personage. When I

first started gardening, particularly between the wars, that was what gardening was, or anyway ninety per cent organic growing, because at that time there weren't the chemicals around that there are these days, the synthetic ones. There were no synthetic fertilisers of the sort that we have been using now. Mind you, I am all in favour of organic gardening, though I don't think you can grow one hundred per cent organically. Some producers can get very close to it, but I don't think they can grow things to the extent that they get one hundred per cent organic. It's not an easy thing to do, and by that I mean it's not an easy thing to convert to – it takes a minimum of three years to convert to organic growing.

'We tried doing this at Springbok. We had to have an outlet for the produce we grew, so we started a farm shop there that my wife used to run. We covered a large area at Springbok. With kitchen garden and glasshouses, there were four-and-half to five acres of vegetables and fruit there, and one of the biggest glasshouses was about a quarter of an acre – big enough to plough and rotavate with a tractor; and there were other houses as well. To try to boost sales we thought we would "go organic". For a start you have to purge your land before you could even think of going organic. We thought the availability of the manure from a milking herd of about 110 cows, plus a beef unit, and huge poultry unit, it would be viable.

'We had the wherewithal to do it, but the trouble was, that what we termed our labour force were only trainees; sometimes that would run at about twenty to twenty-two trainees, at other times, for various reasons, it could drop as low as four. Now, organic growing is very labour-intensive. If, for example, we sowed a crop of carrots, putting in forty rows of carrots across our field, then doing it organically with a twenty-man labour force was quite easy; but if our force dropped to a four-man labour force we had no option but to try to control the weeds and pests in those carrots inorganically. So what happened was, you could go along gaily getting towards your organic goal for a couple of years, but because your labour force fluctuated, bang! In six months it went, because you had to use a spray that you would not have used normally. Yes, you have got to have a large and regular enough labour force to grow organically on a commercial scale. It was not as easy as our committee thought it would be.'

Jim is able to laugh at some mistakes. When they had a pilot scheme to grow 'pick-your-own' strawberries with some 10,000 plants, Jim recommended the ground should be left fallow for a year to clear the ground of weeds. 'No' he was told. 'There's no time for that.' So the 10,000 strawberry plants were put in. 'They grew a treat for a few weeks. Then the following spring the strawberries stood nine to ten inches high and the dock stood about two-and-half feet and growing like rockets! It would have been far better to have put down rhubarb which at least would have covered the weed!'

When Jim was training men at Springbok he had a one hundred per cent public examination pass rate, until the last year, when just one man failed his exams. That man knew it all, he needed no more training. 'I know this backwards. I can do it with my eyes shut.' We have all met that sort at one time or another, so our sympathy can rest with Jim when he says emphatically, *'I could have kicked him!'*

However, Jim is retired now, or semi-retired. He and his wife are resident wardens at one of the Gardener's Royal Benevolent Homes. Jim still gives lectures and judges at horticultural shows for the Royal Horticultural Society, and his great sense of humour enables him to look back upon even the most difficult experiences and see the funny side!

RUN RABBIT RUN

Peter Burd

Dunrobin Castle, Sutherland

'In the old days if a rabbit appeared there was about four or five keepers immediately on the scene. The gardener just phoned the head keeper and the whole lot were down right away. Now the rabbits are just digging the place up,' says Peter Burd. Today at Dunrobin Castle, head gardener Stuart James agrees that they are a major problem. They are still chased personally, but to less effect. 'We use abusive language, we shoot them, we trap them, we gas them, and still they beat us!' They arrive in numbers, burrowing into the hollow centre of the wide old walls and on again into the garden. They slip over gates, and bite through wire netting. 'They are very resilient things, and I feel we are doomed to suffer them. I could have a much lusher garden with far more of the smaller plants, but for them. The herbaceous borders are all dug up in the winter and the roots eaten. I have a corner which I call the rabbit garden, that is my attempt at appeasement. All God's creatures have a place and I'm trying to make this place theirs!'

David Whelan, retired ghillie, with a rabbit snare he made himself

Peter Burd's grandfather was a gardener with the Duke of Sutherland for fifty years. His father went to India to become a tea planter, but returned before Peter was born; later, his death meant that Peter had to leave school suddenly, and in 1934 at the age of fifteen, he was taken on as an apprentice at Dunrobin Castle, the Sutherlands' house at Golspie. 'It was all drawn up – a year in the kitchen garden, a year in the flower or pleasure garden, and a year under glass, then a couple of years both inside and out. And you learnt floristry, and did all the decorating in the castle. There was a foreman in each section. I enjoyed

it. The men you worked with taught you everything they knew. In those days Dunrobin was just turning out apprentices. They applied for jobs, got their references from the head gardener, and if they were lucky, they got a job.'

Peter lived in the bothy where there were four single rooms, and has no complaints about his treatment there. The bothy woman cleaned and cooked hearty meals for them, very basic but adequate, and the castle had electricity from its own plant so they had hot water to fill the tin bath in the scullery. The boys worked from 7am till 12 noon, then from 1pm till 5pm at night; on Saturday mornings they finished at 12 noon. For the first three years of his working life Peter earned 12s 6d, 15s and 18s a week; he had to buy his own clothes for work such as heavy denims and boots, together with wet weather gear. The men wore oilskins, and often got very wet.

'In my first year I helped to supply vegetables to the castle, and wheel them up the castle brae [hill] in wheelbarrows. It took us the whole morning. In those days there were probably about a hundred staff, ninety to a hundred in the servants' hall –

chauffeurs, grooms, ladies' maids and so on. The family might come up in the spring and then for eight to ten weeks in the season, but the staff were permanent.' At Dunrobin they kept very careful accounts, which included records of all the vegetables delivered to the castle, so that they could be priced and the profitability of the gardens assessed. The farm was run in the same way, and it was all worked out to show the return on each section of the estate. 'Wages were so small then, and the vegetables we produced were all prime stuff, it must have been quite a fair return on the labour. Local shops would take the surplus, and they were very keen on that, because there wasn't so much around then. Tomatoes and apples were very easy to get rid of, and plums and pears. We grew rasps and strawberries, currants and everything, and there was plenty of demand for that. The nurseries in Inverness were keen to get flowers too, gladioli and so on.' They also had the usual run of vines, peaches, nectarines, melons, cucumbers, and a flower house growing carnations and chrysanthemums.

Dunrobin Castle is a massive stone structure with towers and turrets, set on a cliff overlooking the sea. The gardens are at sea level and were designed by Sir Charles Barry, probably between 1830 and 1850. The family papers, now in the Scottish National Archive, contain very little detail on the gardens, which were really the nineteenth-century Scottish idea of formal French gardens. The main patterns remain today, that is, belts of evergreen shrubbery flanking three parterres with low box hedges enclosing flowerbeds; they are made to be seen from the castle windows above. Originally, large quantities of bedding plants would have been used, then dahlias in the 1940s and 1950s, changing to roses later on. One of the parterres is circular, which is a rather unusual shape; Stuart James feels that the design may have been inspired by the Scottish targe, or shield. 'They had lots of studs in them for protection, and that is what the yews and aralias represent, I think. Then they had patternwork on them – the L-shapes and the square shapes of the beds, and some of them had a central spike, which our fountain represents.' Large trees and hedge windbreaks intersect the gardens, and the whole is enclosed by high walls. Grassy fields, now no longer mown, lead directly on to the beach. Kitchen garden, glasshouses and garden offices are off to the side and out of sight.

Peter has fond memories of the kitchen garden before the war. 'The kitchen garden was a typical walled, Scottish garden type with borders backed by apple trees or whatever, with flowers in the borders and the vegetables in plots at the back. You see it was quite a display, the old Scottish idea with massive borders of annuals. The vegetables were all screened off, you had to go and look for them. It was very warm and very sheltered. We could grow runner beans quite easily, which are not very easy up here. It was more or less organically grown, perhaps a little fertiliser to boost things if they were a wee bit backward when they were required. The amount of stuff that went in to it, fifty or sixty loads of manure was nothing. We made middens of manure and the mowings and the compost and everything. Quite a strong mixture. Layers and layers one on top of the other. The soil is very sandy. In the kitchen garden we went down about four feet. That was my first experience of trenching about three spades' lengths deep, and the manure was forked into each one. At that time, I was

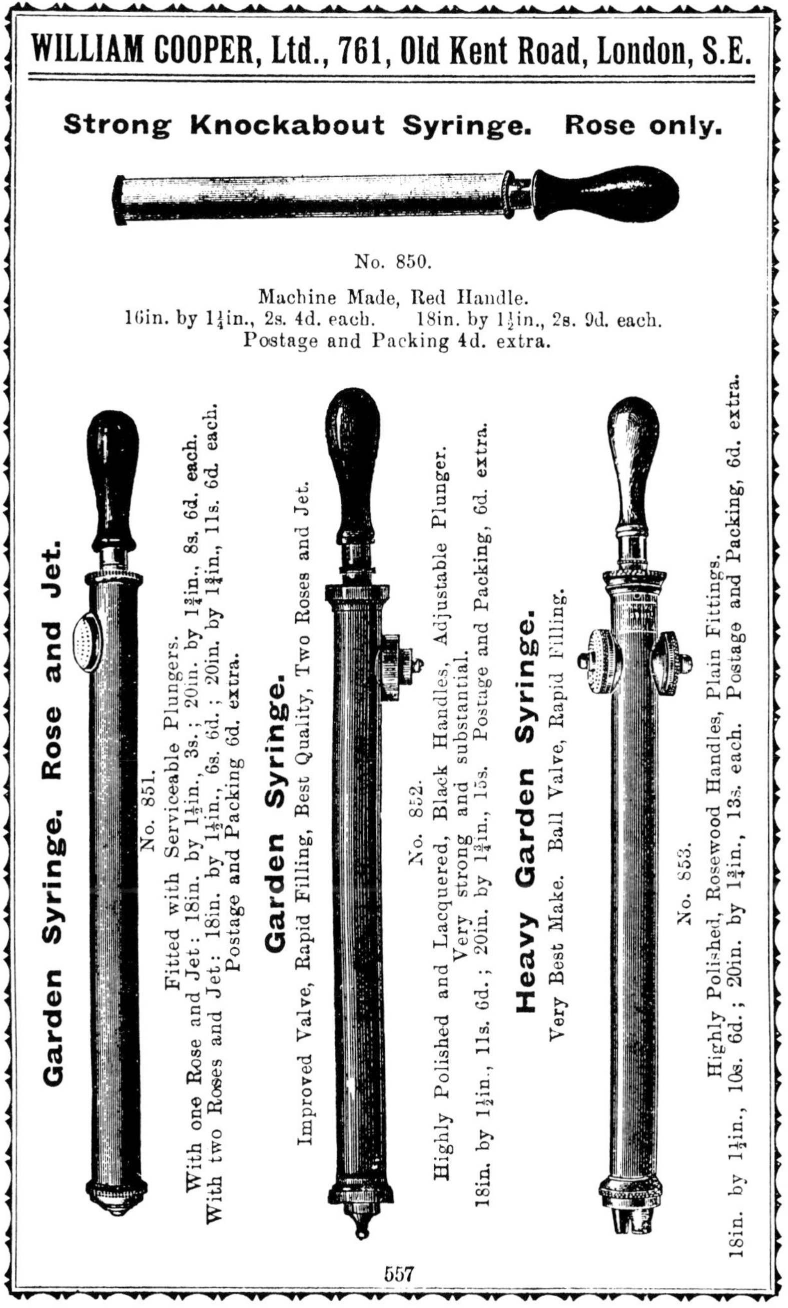

WILLIAM COOPER, Ltd., 761, Old Kent Road, London, S.E.

Strong Knockabout Syringe. Rose only.

No. 850.

Machine Made, Red Handle.
16in. by 1¼in., 2s. 4d. each. 18in. by 1½in., 2s. 9d. each.
Postage and Packing 4d. extra.

Garden Syringe. Rose and Jet.

No. 851.
Fitted with Serviceable Plungers.
With one Rose and Jet: 18in. by 1½in., 3s.; 20in. by 1¾in., 8s. 6d. each.
With two Roses and Jet: 18in. by 1½in., 6s. 6d.; 20in. by 1¾in., 11s. 6d. each.
Postage and Packing 6d. extra.

Garden Syringe.
Improved Valve, Rapid Filling, Best Quality, Two Roses and Jet.

No. 852.
Highly Polished and Lacquered, Black Handles, Adjustable Plunger.
Very strong and substantial.
18in. by 1½in., 11s. 6d.; 20in. by 1¾in., 15s. Postage and Packing, 6d. extra.

Heavy Garden Syringe.
Very Best Make. Ball Valve, Rapid Filling.

No. 853.
Highly Polished, Rosewood Handles, Plain Fittings.
18in. by 1½in., 10s. 6d.; 20in. by 1¾in., 13s. each. Postage and Packing, 6d. extra.

557

about fifteen, I couldn't see over the top of the trench! It grew some good stuff. They don't do that sort of thing nowadays.' Today the kitchen garden is a wilderness, except for the small part which Stuart tends for his personal use. He has renovated some of the glasshouses simply to grow pot plants for the castle.

'I measured the boxwood hedges, and there were two miles of them to cut, by hand of course. Then there were the steep banks up to the castle. A lot of those were scythed, we had no Flymos or anything like that, all hand-scythed, and it's very difficult to stand on a steep bank and do that. Then there was the ivy all round the

terrace. That was a laborious sort of job because the ivy used to give you a terrible rash, almost a dermatitis; though we just carried on.

'I remember one story. The carter was quite a character. He used to pick up all the mowings in the flower garden and outside as well, and once there was a big wasp byke [nest] hanging from one of the terraces, and the man mowing asked him to get it down. He knocked it down, but he was bald and it landed on top of his head!

'They had a nursery garden to propagate all the bedding plants, and grow cut flowers for the house. I remember digging perhaps four thousand cuttings of penstemons, just putting them in frames, done for the borders. The glasshouses were probably the most interesting because it was variety all the time. In the flower house we kept changing the different flowers, all in pots. There was nobody there to see it, but . . .'

In the fourth and fifth years of his apprenticeship, Peter and the other boys were given more responsibility, and opportunity to work on their own. At the end of his apprenticeship in 1939 Peter gained a scholarship to go to Wisley in January 1940. 'I think there was a written part to it, and you had to have five years experience, and the knowledge. Of course the war came, and I never re-applied to them after the war.'

Instead, Peter went to a landscape firm in Edinburgh, which was very successful, and he ended up as the head of a staff of about two hundred. He tired of city life after a few years however, and went to Berkshire. The climate in England makes gardening much easier, so that you can get two crops instead of one, while using the same methods. 'I think that is why Scots gardeners find it so easy to go and work in England, actually!' Then, after trying a market garden in Brora which was under-capitalised, Peter went to Dunvegan Castle in Skye. Here they would transport heavy soil from Ireland, and use coral to lighten it, rotavating them in together; it was apparently quite an experience. And after Skye, Peter went to the Reay Forest near Laxford Bridge, belonging to the Duke of Westminster's estate; but the midges and the rain made it an ordeal to work there. 'We had some stuff made in Norway to counteract the midges, but it used to run down into your face and wasn't worth the bother, really.'

By now it was the mid-1960s and Peter was offered two jobs at the same time, one of which was Inverewe on the west coast of Scotland, where conditions are favourable for many sub-tropical plants. This was where Peter would have preferred to work. For the sake of their children's schooling, however, the Burds moved back to Dunrobin, although Peter himself did not particularly like the formality of the gardens at Dunrobin.

'It was very run down. They were actually planting dahlias about July. Neglect goes very deep, and there was an awful lot to do. There were no properly trained men there after the previous head gardener had died, so I started teaching them the basics. They had turned the castle over to a boys' boarding school at the time and some of the boys used to help, too; for most of them it was just a labour, though one has ended up as a gardener in the south of Scotland. Then they changed again and went commercial, which I'm not very fond of actually, but I had to do it. You know, selling vegetables. We took in a big acreage. I had to contact markets in Glasgow and Edinburgh, four hundred dozen lettuce and this type of thing; and it's all done at night. It was worked from Trentham in Staffordshire, by an accountant there. [Trentham was another Sutherland property.] Everything had to be packaged according to EEC regulations, which is quite a lot of work. The ornamental side of the gardens was open to the public then, too. Unfortunately the custodian in the castle was put in charge of the ornamental side, and I'm afraid I didn't

Peter Burd in 1950

OUTDOOR ROSES, watch as they grow to detect if leaves are curling and aphis forming; if so, wash them with the decoction of Quassia chips previously referred to, strong tobacco water, or one of the numerous forms of prepared insecticide. Owing to the peculiarity of Rose-leaf surfaces, these pests are with difficulty dispelled without a great waste of wash, for which reason an aphis brush, as shown, is very desirable.

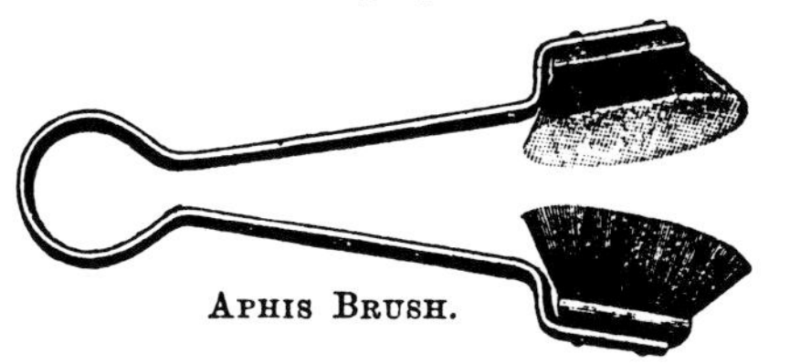
Aphis Brush.

It is preferable to the common ineffectual process of dislodging them with the hand.

approve very much of that. He had no knowledge of it and killed a lot of things, but I just had to accept it.'

Stuart James comments: 'They moved the head gardener on, into the nursery and market garden, in an effort to make the garden pay, and this practically broke him, I think. They missed the point that gardening is an art form, and art seldom ever pays. Well, not till somebody's dead of course!'

Peter had to run the gardens economically, and therefore introduced different plants. 'One that is thriving there I think is *gunnera manicata*. There were some very wet spots in the garden and I got this from a nurseryman in Hawick – if you got this going in a very wet spot it took up all the moisture. It was difficult moneywise to get anything done and it's quite limited what you can do really, when it all boils down to cash.' They planted roses in the beds among the formal box hedges, and they were quite effective. They lasted about ten years, but then they had to change the soil and flowers completely as sickness developed when new roses were planted again in the same place. They had plenty of leaf mould and compost, and were still able to obtain some cow manure from the farmyard, and seaweed was brought by horse and cart from the beach to be mixed with the leaf mould.

When Peter was running the kitchen gardens on a commercial basis during the 1960s, he had new glasshouses and ten tunnels about 120 feet long which produced peppers, cucumbers, and celery as well as the lettuce. 'There was a good body in the soil, and we moved the tunnels round. We grubbed a lot of the trees out, so that we could use equipment there. We had a tractor and rotavator, and all the modern seed precision machines for sowing maybe two-and-a-half acres of carrots – the biggest job was lifting them!' From the two men there when he arrived, Peter's staff increased to a dozen. 'I had two very reliable women in the tunnels, you could just put them to a job and leave them at it; they were far better than the men. The men, well, they might break the tools, then the job stops. Most of them were all right but you just had to tone them down a bittie sometimes; they got a bit too enthusiastic. For instance, they saw something once on television, where they were showing how to snap off the tomatoes. I'd been away, and when I came back it was like a blinking desert! I had an awful job to bring the whole crop back. But they'd seen it on TV and thought I was old-fashioned. Sometimes these TV programmes are not the best, you need to know what you are doing. This time it made the stuff unsaleable, all spotted, and the

inspectors who watch your produce, we got complaints from them. The men would listen, but things happen when you're out of sight.'

Peter remembers with pleasure the times before the war when he had to decorate the dining-room. 'We had a flower room way down in the basement of the castle. You had to be out by ten in the morning, from the main rooms. Every day we went up with sheets, we had to take off our boots so we didn't make a mark where the housemaids had brushed. There were no hoovers or anything like that. Talking about vases, they would finish up about eight or ten feet high, and big ornamental screens of sweet-scented verbena, all placed in the corridor where you could scent them going past. And the finger bowls on the table were all with sprigs of verbena and so on – and the dinner tables. They were charged twenty-five guineas a time, charged against labour and flowers. A dinner table finished was really lovely to look at, the silver and plate, and the four pipers. Sometimes they would have a councillors' dinner, for about two hundred. And the foresters and gardeners, if they wanted to earn a pound or two, they could cart the stuff up to the waiters. The kitchen was quite a long way away. Quite a few chickens and lobsters and so on, and some went missing!'

Stuart James, the head gardener today, trained at Nottingham and worked at Langwell in Berriedale before coming to Dunrobin. His boss is Lord Strathnaver, who will eventually succeed to the title. 'He takes a personal interest in the garden, so between us we decide what the aims are and what we should do. It makes all the difference, that he likes it, otherwise you'd be in the wilderness a little bit, because it isn't your own garden; although in some ways as head gardener you treat it as being your own, and you certainly commit yourself to it, and indeed come to love it. But as you don't hold the purse strings, without personal interest from the owner, you are very limited as to what you can actually achieve.'

One problem not yet solved concerns the ponds at the centres of the parterres which suffer from growths of algae, particularly bad in sunny summers when the sun reacts with the nitrates in the water. 'We've tried the rotten straw method. Putting rotten straw in the water supply, the toxins are meant to combat the algae, but it

didn't work for us, and it was unsightly. My latest idea is to plant up the reservoir where the headwater is held with reeds and bulrushes, because these plants actually sieve out the nitrates, but I don't know enough about it yet. What we don't want to be doing is to be putting chemical treatments in it, because all the water just ends up in the sea.' The use of chemicals, fertilisers and weedkillers is in fact minimal all over the garden.

The raised shrub border gives an altogether different atmosphere to the gardens, one of relaxation and informality. 'I feel that this marks Dunrobin out,' says Stuart. 'It has grown into its Scottish self. If you like, it is the rather relaxed frame to the garden. Many visitors comment on it. It is nice to see the formal gardens plus something that is a little more easy on the eye; you can sit amongst it in repose.'

The large mixed border at the bottom of the terrace is very colourful, consisting of mixed shrubs and herbaceous flowers. The fuchsia, 'Dunrobin Bedder,' was bred here by a previous head gardener called Melville, who also bred a snowdrop 'Melvillii,' now lost to the estate. The border does not, however, have a strong overall design, probably because details have been altered over the years, and Stuart hopes to work a new design before too long. Shortage of labour, of course, means that many

of his projects have to be postponed indefinitely. Another splash of colour is provided by the border leading towards the Westminster gates, which are a wonderful example of ironwork. This border is backed by pleached limes.

As head gardener today, Stuart James sums up his position: 'Compared to my predecessor I am so well off, but there is always more, more, more. Maintenance is a bit like a strait jacket, either you are strapped in by it, or you lose what you have worked so hard to establish.'

Like Peter, Stuart enjoys feeding his plants. 'I've got two bins for the compost, I don't know how many cubic metres it is. We believe in it. The first year, when we hadn't got the compost systems going, we had a storm which minced up the seaweed on the beach and we spent a week with tractor, trailer and barrows, collecting it. Getting access to the beach is a problem with the tractor. You need a fantastic bulk, too, it just melts away. That compost bin is largely herbaceous stuff; this one is basically leaves and grass cuttings, a bit of lime and a little bit of fertiliser, and give it a watering. And it comes out lovely stuff. I really like that bit of the job. It's the mucky end, but it's very, very satisfying, I think, because it's wholesome, and it's good to be doing it, and the ground looks good when it's covered with it. I began to see stuff responding after a couple of years of using it.'

It is remarkable how both Peter Burd and Stuart James come back to the same conclusion – the importance and the pleasure of working with good organic material.

Stuart James at Dunrobin in 1993

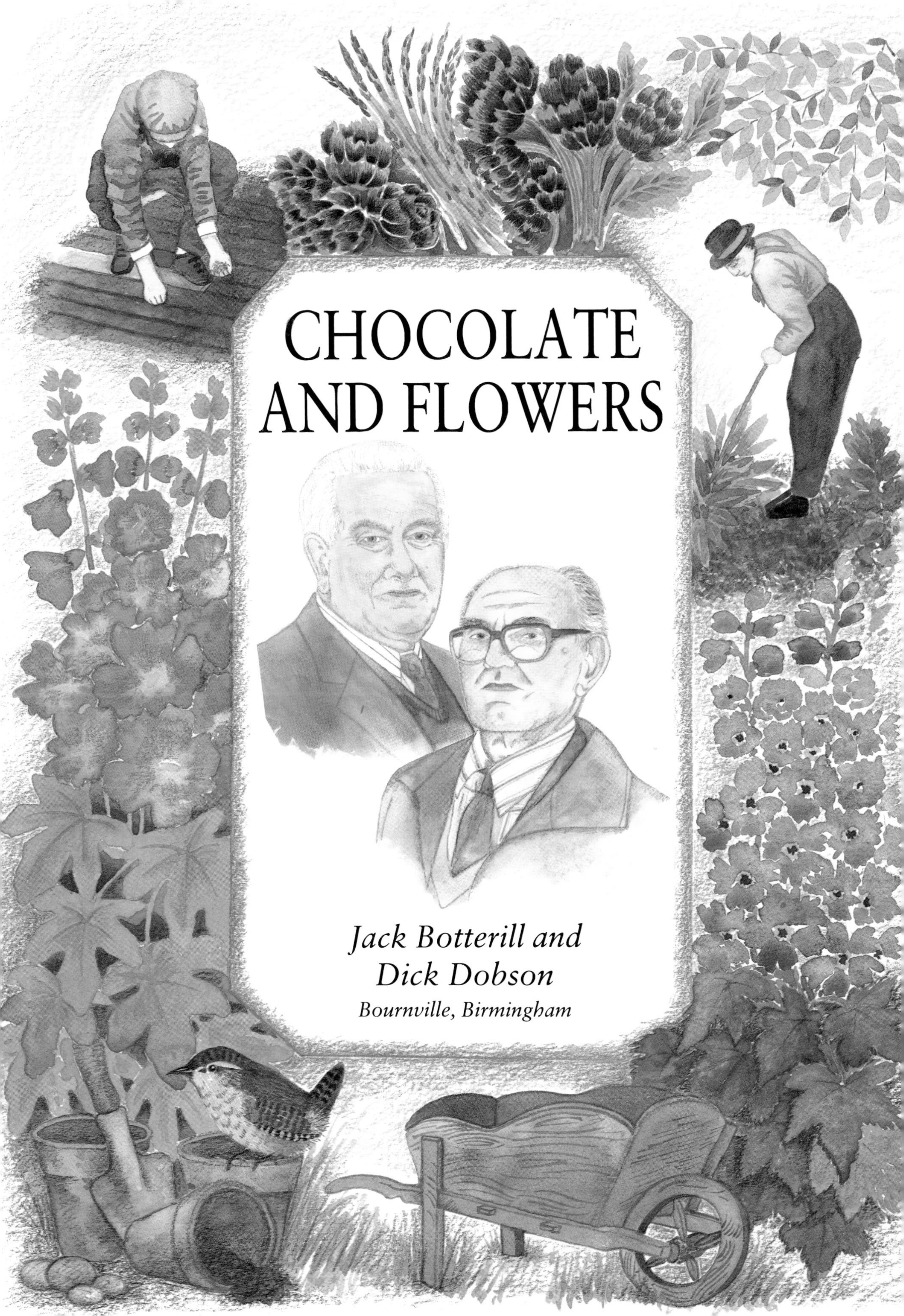
CHOCOLATE
AND FLOWERS
Jack Botterill and
Dick Dobson
Bournville, Birmingham

'Well, if I can get into Bournville, I'm made!' so said Jack Botterill, when he saw an advertisement for the job of gardener at the Cadbury's factory outside Birmingham. It was known that they were very good to their employees, looking after them well, with good sports facilities, subsidised canteen food, generous pensions and other perks. The job paid £8 a week, which was lower than the factory workers received, but Jack thought it was sufficient in 1949 when he was not long out of the army. It was enough for him to start buying a house, anyway (take-home pay £6 10s a week, mortgage £8 2s per month). Jack says of Cadbury's: 'They wanted people to feel that they were part of the company family. I think I felt that. They were happy days.' Dick came to Cadbury's a few years after Jack; he had been trained as a gardener at Shifnal, near where he was born in Shropshire, where his starting wage in 1932 was 6s a week.

There was a very strict hierarchy in those days among the sixty-two gardeners who worked at Bournville in the 1950s; they started at the bottom on the unskilled flat rate, moving through semi-skilled to skilled, with no bonuses. There was a file report on each man, and he would be assessed by the manager and foreman every year to enable him to make a move to the next grade when the time came. Nothing official would be discussed, the employee would simply receive a letter through the post to inform him of his new wages. At the beginning 'You started with a broom and shovel, sweeping the leaves. After a bit, you got rid of your broom and shovel and got a pair of secateurs. When you had a pair of secateurs, that was it, you were then known as a gardener!'

Dick worked in the kitchen garden, where they used to grow espalier trees and fans. He remembers the Blenheim apple trees which must have been a hundred years old then. These apples have very good keeping qualities, and will keep from one year to the next. 'We've had two ton of apples off those six trees; and the pears, Pitmaston Duchess, we've weighed them at 1lb each.'

The kitchen garden and greenhouse complex used to be part of Bournbrook Hall. The house was demolished when the site was bought for Cadbury's, though these outbuildings remained. Once, part of the orchard subsided and they discovered the brickwork of the old laundry underground. It had to be filled with rubble and covered over again.

Some produce was grown in the kitchen garden, but Dick remembers mostly flowers. Some of the roses and other blooms which they grew were given to photographers to take pictures to adorn the chocolate box lids; then every girl that got married was presented with a carnation and a bible, and another flower was given on leaving the firm. The carnations were grown in the greenhouses, where Dick also worked. Bouquets of flowers were used regularly to decorate the offices of senior personnel in the works; it was said that in 1932, 4,500 vases of flowers had been used in the factory – for instance 300 indoor chrysanthemum plants had been grown, giving 2,500 blooms. Although by the 1950s the scale was not the same, floral decorations were still ordered every day, and Dick, who had been trained in this work in his previous employment, loved doing them. Special arrangements were called for when there were unusual events or occasions, such as the centenary

celebrations in 1979 held to mark the move to Bournville. Then there were official visits to the factory, and garden parties, and events at the Almshouses or College of Education; all these called for extra efforts on the part of the gardeners. The greenhouses would also produce hundreds of bedding plants, either from seed or grown from cuttings. Geraniums and cineraria were popular, cyclamen and carnations, and many others.

Dick used to work on the tomato plants in the greenhouse – hundreds of these, too; some went to the canteen and others would be sold. They used to make all their own leaf mould for the tomato pots. They had five bays to contain the mould, and it would be turned over from one bay to the next every year, so that the one they used was five years old; and then they filled up the first one again. 'It was beautiful stuff.' They put their own soil and John Innes in to the mixture, filled the pots and put them in the steriliser. All the greenhouses would be washed down every winter with soft soap. The greenhouse staff in Dick's early days would not allow the outside staff to go through the houses 'or only when everything was cleared. You weren't allowed to see or touch; I think it was sacred ground to them. An outside man was a nobody.'

In the 1950s, the gardener's day started at 7.42am and finished at 4.54pm, and the hour was divided into six minute slots; lunch was an hour's break from 12.18pm. They were allowed a tea-break in the morning, but not in the afternoon; this ruling was ignored, however, and the kettle would be boiled up behind some bushes, or if that was not practicable, a hole would be dug and the stove lit below ground level, out of sight of the prowling foreman. At dinner time in the middle of the day, the men went either to the canteen if they were working in that area, or they would go to their mess room. 'They had a row of bowls to wash in, and that was luxury; the old ones used to tell us that they had had a bucket. They were always saying that we were living in a time of luxury.' A donkey jacket, overalls and clogs were supplied by the company, though Jack could never get on with the clogs, and used to wear his own safety shoes.

One perk was the holiday allowance. Gardeners were allowed a fortnight's holiday after twelve months, and were given £3 for each child and £5 for the wife.

Bournville's first motor mower, sold to Cadbury's in 1902, seen here on the Men's Recreation Ground. The driver is Ben Florence, head groundsman until 1920 (Cadbury Ltd)

The company could also be very generous when it came to helping with the children's education. When Jack's son got into King Edward's School: 'He had to have a lot of uniform, and to get a complete outfit all at once, well, on our wages you couldn't do it. I went to the office and they gave me all these forms to fill in, and I am sorry to say that I hate forms – I would do anything to get out of them. But I did it, and gave them back, and a fortnight later I got a cheque which practically paid for all the uniform.'

The grounds which they had to look after consisted of all the areas round the factory. The Men's Recreation Ground was overlooked by the canteen, and dominated on the road side by the huge pavilion; the Girls' Grounds were situated on the other side of the road and dated from the time when the sexes were segregated. The Grounds were reached by a tunnel going under the road. Senior staff would chaperon the girls from their place of work, down the corridors, outside and through the tunnel to take the air in their designated place away from the corrupting influence of the men. There were lawns surrounded by trees and shrubs for seclusion; a pond formed from the cellars of the demolished Bournbrook Hall, and a pergola screening a stage for performances of concerts and plays. There was also a croquet lawn, and many flowerbeds which have long since been turfed over to save costs.

Some distance away, seventy-five acres of land had been purchased at Rowheath to provide sports fields and other leisure amenities, including nine acres devoted to the gardening club. The club had worked well in the first half of the century; it was held three evenings a week and on Saturdays with the purpose of helping youngsters to learn to tend a garden. Seeds and tools were bought in bulk with consequent savings, and lecturers were invited to share their expertise. After the war, however, most of those who came were older people, primarily looking for bargains, and interest in the club gradually waned. Rowheath also boasted a lake, lawns and flowerbeds which fronted another pavilion large enough to stage events. (This whole area has now passed out of the hands of Cadbury's; some sporting facilities are left, but they are run by the Bournville Trust, and some of the land has been sold for development.)

Jack Botterill liked to work in the area around the director's offices, feeling that everybody got to know you there. 'The Cadburys used to take a lot of interest in what was going on in the garden, and I think they used to respect who you were, whoever you were.' By Mr John Cadbury's office there were flowerbeds, window-boxes and a rockery and there were always masses of spring bulbs. It caused a rumpus when the holly hedge was cut down from about ten foot to a neat three, but after a while it was agreed that it was much better kept that way – they could see out of the windows!

Both Jack and Dick feel that they had happy years at Bournville. They enjoyed themselves at work; they had to work hard and the discipline was strict, but they respected this attitude. Mr Neales, who was the head gardener through the 1950s, might call someone into the office to give them a good dressing-down, but then it was finished. For example, Jack's friend, Walter, was always smoking, and they weren't allowed to smoke on the job. Once Jack saw Mr Neales coming (he always rode a push-bike with a basket on the front) and warned Walter to put his cigarette out; thinking he had gone past, Walter started up again, when a voice came over the hedge, 'Walter, you're smoking!' 'No, I'm not, Mr Neales' said Walter, as he ground

his cigarette into the mud. At dinner time there was trouble: 'I caught you this morning, Walter.' 'Yes it was a bloody Player and all!' Mr Neales, having made his point, finished the incident, 'Well, you'd better have one of mine then.'

When Neales retired in 1958, the system began to change. The next man had not been trained as a professional gardener; he was easygoing and pleasant, but introduced new ideas such as labelling for the plants: 'He can't remember the names!' and 'It looks like a bloody cemetery!' were typical of the comments. During the 1960s, the manpower had been reduced to about thirty-five to forty gardeners, still doing the same jobs as before but aided by better machinery. Then in the 1970s came the merger with Schweppes; a new director came round and said, 'Very nice, but it's all gold plate, and the best thing to do is to get rid of gold plate.' Eventually the much reduced gardens and grounds were run by office staff.

'We hardly ever saw them,' said Dick. 'And it's hard work working with somebody who isn't a gardener. You've got to tell them everything, and if you want to buy something, you've got to explain why.' Jack, having started at the bottom as a labourer, got to the top of the department as acting manager. When the head

Dick Dobson picking Pitmaston Duchess pears at Bournville (Cadbury Ltd)

Jack Botterill outside the director's office in 1955 (Cadbury Ltd)

gardener left in 1982, the department was put under the control of Lodges and Security and Jack moved up, but without the old dignified title. 'The first Christmas I had to budget for the next year. I'd never done this before and hadn't got a clue. "Well, how many tools do you want?" I rubbed my hands with glee, and was asking everyone else. "Oh," they said "you want to get so many spades and so many forks." I gave the list back to the boss and the phone went about an hour later. "You've got to cut this by half Jack, it's far too much, you can't have all this, you know." So the next year I thought I'd double it. "Oh Jack, you can't have all this, you must cut it by half." That's fair enough, I'm going to get what I want then. The next year he didn't wear it at all. "You pulled a fast one last year. You'll sit here and do it with me now."'

When they next asked for a redundancy, Jack, as the oldest man, decided to take it. He had worked for Cadbury's for more than thirty years, but the job had changed radically during the previous decade and as acting manager he was working seven days a week. He has no regrets, it was time for him to go.

The company was started by a young man of twenty-two running a single-handed grocery business in Birmingham. John Cadbury's firm prospered during the nineteenth century, and it was his son George who, in 1879, moved the company to Bournville. His vision of the future was revolutionary at the time: it included not just the factory on a green field site, but also the provision of housing for all grades of his employees in a healthy environment – his workers should not continue to live in the slums of inner city Birmingham. His vision, successfully put into action, inspired many, and led to other experiments of the same kind. By 1900, more than three hundred houses had been built with educational and leisure facilities to go with them, and George Cadbury transferred the property to an independent body, the Bournville Village Trust, renouncing all financial interest in the project. 'The founder is desirous of alleviating the evils which arise from the insanitary and insufficient accommodation supplied to large numbers of the working classes, and of securing to the workers in factories some of the advantages of outdoor village life, with opportunities for the natural and healthful occupation of cultivating the soil.'

Each house had an ample plot of its own, made ready for the occupant to grow his own vegetables and flowers, and a fruit tree was planted in each. The various trees at the bottom of the garden provided some privacy and looked very pleasant. A lawn was provided for children's play and family relaxation, and hedges were put in place. In the early years, when some of the occupants could be expected to have little experience of gardening, competitions were started to help raise awareness. Gardening associations were formed originally as co-operative groups, buying equipment and sundries and exchanging ideas and information. The resulting competitions were very popular. To give some scale of the proceedings in 1906, judging took place among a hundred and twelve kitchen gardens, five hundred flower gardens and seventy boys' and girls' gardens. (This continues today in the form of the Bournville Village Festival. Garden classes are restricted to Bournville residents. They also have children's events unconnected with gardening.)

In the early 1930s, individual gardens were written up in the *Bournville Works Magazine*. Mr G. Pickett's garden, for instance, featured a small thatched summer

house, three ponds with fountains, each containing rare lilies, a rockery with choice alpines, mature fruit trees, 350 roses, stone benches, a sundial and dove-cot with doves. In contrast, at the beginning of the war, an article in the magazine started with an exhortation to 'everyone to make the most of his land', with hints on how to grow a series of vegetables to provide food throughout the year. The company grounds, with the notable exception of the Men's Recreation Ground, were dug up for the same purpose. When life settled down after the war, it can be seen that the tradition of gardening was well established, both on an individual basis, and from the point of view of appreciating the factory gardens and communal playing fields.

Dick Dobson and Jack Botterill continued the tradition, having been trained before the war and starting with the company soon afterwards. Calvin Green came to Cadbury's in the 1960s, transferring to the greenhouses because of his asthma. As a young man, the complex seemed very large and elaborate to him and he remembers the constant need to stoke the boilers. 'We had to shovel coal in twice a day . . . and wash pots and generally tidy up. I just got menial tasks because I was not expecting to stay long – chop up old turfs, and line the bottom of the pots with horse manure, by hand. We potted these chrysanths on, grew them up in the ashes, and then brought them in for the winter, for the offices as required.' He also had to water the concrete

Jack (left) selling spring flowers to office girls in the 1960s (Cadbury Ltd)

to make a humid atmosphere for the plants. There were six greenhouses and four gardeners working there, doing a great deal of propagation. Unfortunately the greenhouses were set on fire by vandals in 1993 and the whole set have had to be demolished.

Calvin later went to college to train to be a groundsman. In earlier days, all the gardeners had learnt on the job, the older men showing the youngsters by example. Earlier still, there are records showing that apprentices were sent to events such as the Chelsea Flower Show as part of the learning process; yet in all Jack Botterill's career with Cadbury's, he had only a couple of days away for the company (he went to a show set up in Ipswich by Ransomes). For Calvin, who is now head gardener, the situation has been rather different: employees must be trained in specialist work such as using sprays and pesticides, and shown the correct way to handle new machinery. In recent years it has been the policy to move the groundsmen around to familiarise them with each and every aspect of the work, rather than giving them one area to look after, as was the case in Dick Dobson's day.

There are now few ornamental areas, and those that there are, are low cost, low maintenance gardens. The emphasis is on sporting facilities, although these too are much reduced in number. What there are however, are kept in very good condition, so much so that professional teams have played on them: Aston Villa have trained on the football pitches and the Indian team have used a cricket field. Hockey and tennis, and both lawn and crown bowls are among the sports still played today. Previously, if you wanted to play a particular sport, then the company would try to provide it for you.

The young people's welfare was considered to be a matter of legitimate concern to their elders. Ken Sale, one of Calvin's three assistants, went into the gardens as a young man in 1957. He remembers his personal talk with the foreman every six months, when he would be asked what he did in the evenings. He replied that he went to his church youth club, which was a satisfactory answer – he was off the streets. 'We were encouraged to participate. If you were doing nothing, they tended to say "How about doing this section, what do you like?" In those days we had our own dining-room, the youths from fifteen to eighteen. No one else could go in, not girls or older men, about five hundred youths, all together.' Earlier still, boys had had to do PT and swimming, and in the men's pool they did not wear costumes. The girls had their own separate gym and swimming pool and were given uniform swimming costumes on arrival.

For Calvin and Ken, March is the busiest time of year with the changeover from winter to summer sports. Areas of high usage, like the bowling greens or cricket pitches, need top dressing, fertilising and special cutting. Disease control is important, for this may follow on from the special treatments that these turfed areas receive. Today the groundsmen have a tractor which pulls six different kinds of mower. Other equipment includes a huge stiff brush (which was originally made of whalebone, but now comes in plastic), used to remove the worm casts and to stand the grass up for cutting; a big cane to disperse heavy dew – a telescopic aluminium tube 7ft long with a flexible fibreglass end which is 6ft long. When Calvin came in the

Ken Sale (left) and Calvin Green with the Dennis lawn mower

1960s they were still using a Greens motor mower made in the early 1920s. It had been given a new lease of life in 1957 when the Dorman engine and gearbox had been replaced with a Ford engine and gearbox. It was then used as a roller on the Men's Recreation Ground. Cadbury's also had one of the first Land-Rovers off the assembly line at this period, for pulling the gang mowers; for the same job at Rowheath, it was two horses with cloths tied round their hooves so as not to damage the turf.

Barry Lynock took charge of the gardens in 1991, taking over a very different

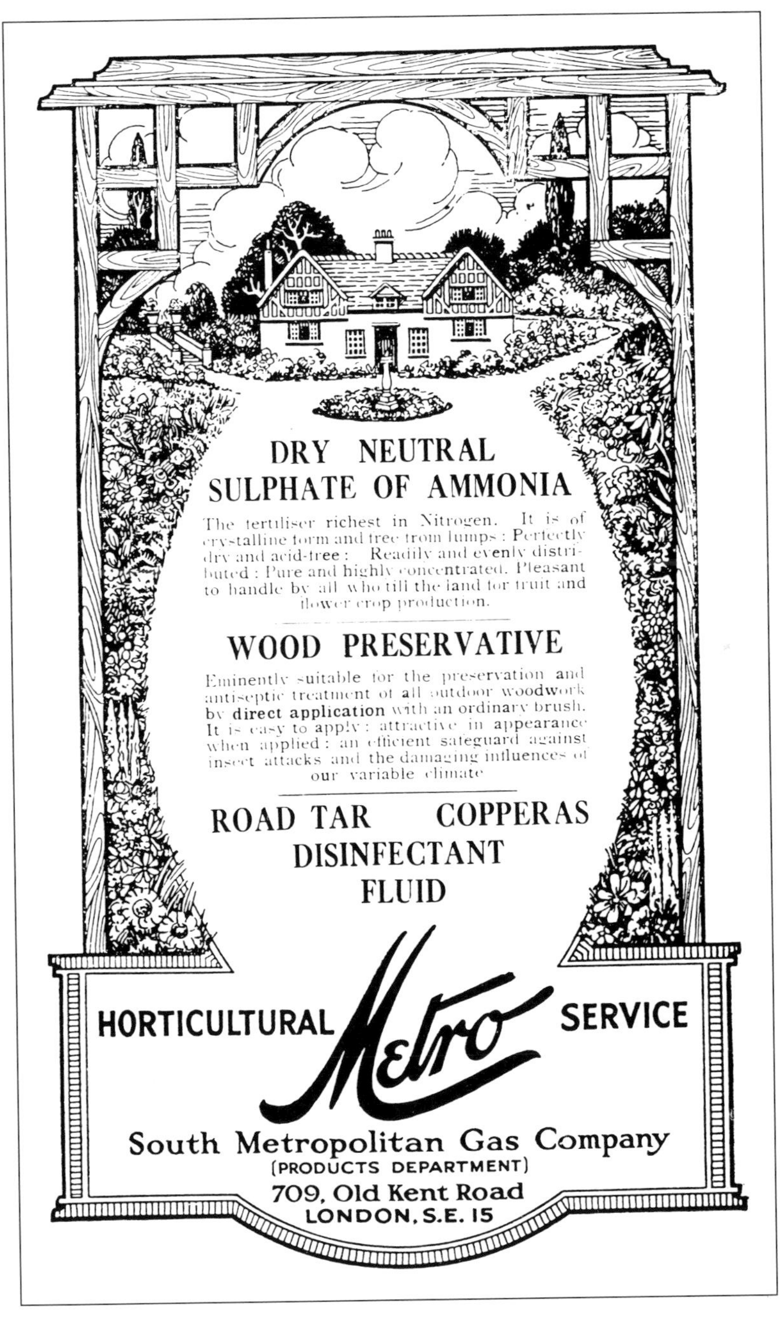

situation from the one which Jack Botterill had known more than forty years previously. Barry has a budget which covers the salaries of his four groundsmen; they do all they can, and specialist work such as major tree surgery or large spraying jobs will go out to contractors. The sporting facilities have to be self-financing.

Previously the company had been paternalistic towards its employees, its ethos to develop the whole person, mind and body, looking after them, and guiding them. This was a philanthropic attitude at the beginning of the century, but is wholly unacceptable in today's world. As Barry points out, 'All of a sudden, the youngsters who were born in the 1940s became very affluent in the 1960s, and they were buying first of all scooters, then it was cars. By the time the next generation came along, what we had demanded of our fathers became the norm. The motor car became very easily accessible, public transport became a lot better, so therefore there was no longer the necessity for people who were looking for jobs to look inward in their own little community. They could get out. And once they had got married or whatever, they weren't looking for houses where they actually worked.' In addition to this social change, when the company became Cadbury Schweppes in the 1970s, it had to be responsible to the shareholders and the concept of benevolent paternalism had to go.

The gardens at Bournville were designed with a very specific purpose in mind, not to please just one family but to provide a healthy environment for the work and leisure of the employees. To this end, they were actively encouraged to make full use of the grounds. Today it is a matter of choice whether an individual uses the facilities which, although much reduced, are still a great pleasure and asset.

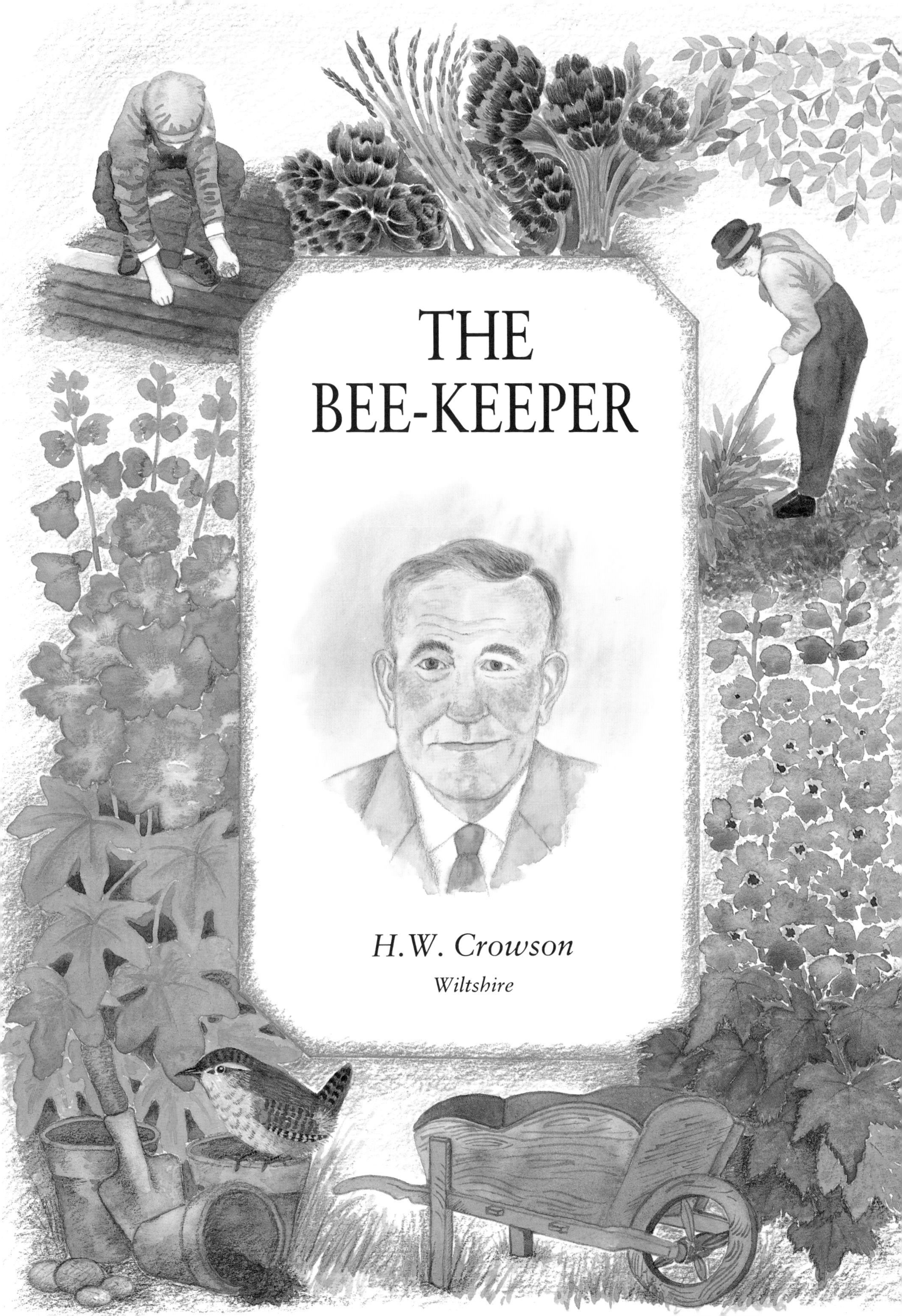

THE BEE-KEEPER

H.W. Crowson

Wiltshire

The Orchid House at Kew Gardens

Mr Crowson was born in Chelsea in 1899, the middle boy of three. His father was a policeman, and his grandfather, who lived in Norfolk, worked as a coal-higgler, as it was known at that time – that is, he went to the pithead at the colliery at Whitwick and collected the coal to be taken back to Shepshed, where he lived, to be delivered locally.

The young Crowson family first lived in Chelsea, a short walk from the Thames, and then they moved to Richmond, near to Kew Gardens. Mr Crowson remembers the orchards, long since gone, going down to Mortlake. Then in 1906 the boys' mother died and family life was disrupted for a while; but their father cared for the three boys, and perhaps thinking their time should be used sensibly, allotted each of them a piece of land in their long narrow garden. '"Now this is your piece of land and I want you to keep it tidy" he said, and that was the beginning of my being interested in gardening. "What shall I plant?" I thought. So I went down the road to the house where I was sometimes sent to buy pot-herbs [as root vegetables for the stewpot, carrots, turnips, parsnips and so on, were always called in those days], and when they had topped and tailed the veggies, I planted these – with the moisture they started to grow and made a pretty fine picture.'

Even as a boy, young Crowson found plants and, more particularly, bees fascinating and he had a friend at school who sat next to him who shared his interest; in fact this friend grew up to make his fortune as the largest bee-keeper in Britain. Mr Crowson did not make a lot of money, but he is content to have earned enough to have given his daughter a good education. As boys, in the winter he and his friend would tuck their tuppenny exercise books under their arms and go off to Kew Gardens. 'It was free then. Well, it was a National Park really. We just wanted to go somewhere in the warm. The keeper with his pill-box hat would come out of his hut to see who it was; we took no notice of him and he took no notice of us, but we did know how to behave ourselves. We learned quite a lot about horticulture that way.'

Mr Crowson senior retired to Marlborough; he had married again, and soon set about having a house of their own built by a builder friend. 'There was a lot of building going on in those days. Father arranged the garden and us boys had to help, cutting grass with sheep-shears, weeding and planting fruit trees.'

Young Crowson also got a job out of school hours helping two ladies who ran a ladies' shop where they sold underwear and so on. He went in at 8am: 'First, I had to clear the rubbish left by the cats. They fed all the cats in the neighbourhood and I had to wash the plates under the cold water tap in the yard. It used to smell terrible! The rubbish had to be put in the dustbins and the front windows wiped over, and there was a brass plate to be cleaned.' Then at 8.50am he would run down to school.

'Dinner time was midday until one o'clock and they used to have a lot of post; I would fold the brown paper and twist the string around so they could use it again. They had a garden away from the shop down the lane and I had to help there, too; it was full of ground elder and red currant bushes and that. I turned a hand there, and ran any errand needed. I would go again in the evening and get their coals up and see to anything else they wanted. I got 1s 3d a week, which wasn't bad because you could get a suit of clothes for a boy for 10s 6d in those days.'

Mr Crowson's interest in bees was aroused when, during his childhood, he went to stay with his aunt for a holiday and met a head gardener who kept bees in the grounds of the big house where he worked. He gave the lad a pot of honey, and this got Mr Crowson started on a hobby that was later to become his profession. He remembered the holiday well: 'In the same village there lived two brothers: Leigh, was their name, and there was a sister. They were nurserymen in a small way, and they used to advertise in *The Smallholder* magazine, plants; say, ten pansies for a shilling. Postage and all would be included. Ten of this and ten of that.'

Mr Crowson's aunt kept the village post office. 'They used to come in with these little parcels of plants that would be sent off at night tied up in newspaper with string and raffia. They put so many stamps on, however much it was. Probably only threepence. That was part of their living, and they did it all for a shilling.'

The Leighs also kept bees; they had allotments at one end of the village and kept their hives there. 'The honey was stored in the shed down there. One day they went down with their horse and cart to collect the honey and when they got there, the bees had found it and taken it all back to their hives. Terrific robbers they are.'

Years later, young Crowson was called up for army service, and he served in World War I; when he returned to the countryside of Wiltshire he took up bee-keeping seriously and started his own apiary, producing honey and also breeding queen bees.

During the war there had been a shortage of queen bees, so Mr Crowson decided to rear them commercially for the wholesale and retail trade, and supplied one of the bee firms. To generate new queens a few combs are taken out, isolating a little of each brood and leaving the queen behind. Deprived of their queen, the worker bees choose a young princess to take her place; they cherish and feed her with royal jelly, the purist and richest nourishment, specially distilled and reserved for her use alone, so she will develop into a queen who will produce young worker eggs. Thus, tiny new colonies are formed. But in order to raise queens, the bee-keeper has, therefore, effectively to destroy his own colonies, breaking them up into smaller units, and this had to be taken into consideration when fixing the price, because the bee-keeper as well as the bee firms had to make a profit.

Once the queen is established and mature, the colony can develop. The sole reason for the existence of the male drones is for one act of love. The weather must be calm for the drones to meet the queen for mating purposes. For her nuptial flight she will choose her time, between midday and four in the afternoon, on a warm and calm sunny day, to soar to a height that no other bees will ever reach in their life. A region is selected that is central to several hives. Nature has taken extraordinary measures to favour the union of males with females of a different stock: hundreds of drones live in each of the neighbouring hives and they will fly over the chosen area; the virgin queen will then choose and wed just one from her myriad suitors.

Very few people have witnessed a queen bee's wedding, but Mr Crowson was once aware that mating was taking place, high above a park close to his home. He discovered that this particular area in Wiltshire was central to commercial apiaries and villages, and to his apiary too, so the bees did not have far to go. He heard the noise made by the bees and recognised it as an accompaniment to mating, and connected it with the area and the time: 'One day I heard a terrific noise over a park where I lived, which I knew to be the sound of drones. High above was a congregation of bees. I couldn't see anything because they were so high up, but it was during this time that the young queens mated. I wrote about it [in beekeeping magazines], but they didn't believe me.'

Later Mr Crowson went to live in Selborne, in Hampshire, and it was here in September, at the end of the season, that he saw another congregation of drones gather way above the oak trees of High Wood. It is more usual for a mating congregation to occur in summer when the bees swarm; however, Mr Crowson found the event had also been witnessed in this area by Gilbert White who recorded it in his writings about Selborne in the mid-eighteenth century (see page 122).

Mr Crowson often wrote articles for the *British Bee Journal*; he recorded this experience, too, and felt rather hurt when he was not at first believed. Nevertheless, the Bee Research Association got in touch with him, and in June sent two men to listen to the congregation. They were impressed, and suggested a virgin queen should be presented for mating, attached to a fishing line, fed from a reel and carried up by a balloon. Unfortunately Mr Crowson could not agree to do this, as he was only an employee there at the time; in those days it would no doubt have been inappropriate to seek permission for such a stunt, and his employer might have taken a dim view of such an experiment. Later, however, one of the men, the editor of the association's magazine at that time, returned with photographs and Mr Crowson's point was proven: the photographs showed a queen being let up on a balloon above a wood, of a drone circling around, and mating taking place.

'It proved my point and his as well. He also found other places where this happened, one being the Isle of Man. It was fascinating.'

Mr Crowson became very interested in diseases of bees, and a local doctor gave him a microscope; this he found very useful, particularly when his bees contracted a disease and he tried to find out more about it. He became so interested that he started

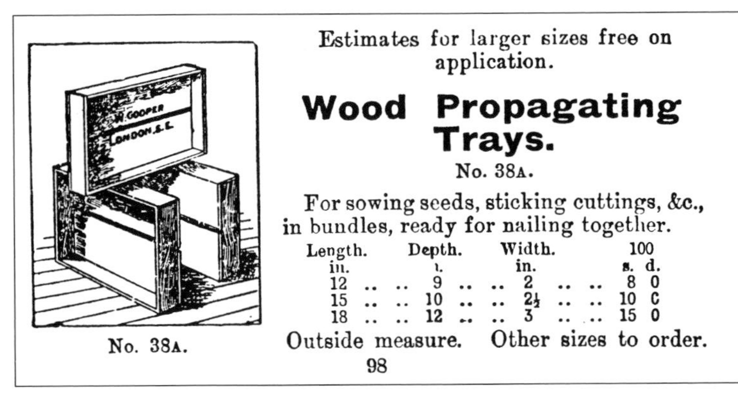

to correspond with the Scottish Agricultural Society on bee diseases. There are many diseases and parasites that attack bees, and some are difficult to cure. *Acarine* is a mite, sometimes known as Isle of Wight disease because it was thought to have originated there. In 1910, it swept viciously across the country, virtually wiping out the indigenous British black bee. It is the colour of bees that indicates their place of origin; to prevent the spread of disease, certain restrictions are placed on the import and export of bees. However, queens of the yellow Italian bee species have been imported for many decades as this strain is more prolific, stronger, more active and gentler than our own. Nonetheless, although the yellow strain is used more widely, it is thought there are pockets where the black bee continues to breed, and some breeders still specialise in breeding them for those who feel our indigenous population of bees should be encouraged.

At first it was thought nothing could be done to combat infection with acarine: the mite goes from the old to the young bees attacking the trachea and infecting the respiratory system; this weakens the bees which crawl out of the hive to die. Bees then come from other apiaries and plunder the infected hive for the spoils – but of course they, too, become infected and so whole colonies are wiped out. Thus the bee-keeper would suffer very badly should his entire apiary be attacked. Many attempts have been made to find a way to eradicate the mite: Mr Crowson used to put a pad soaked with petrol on top of the hive, and it was hoped that this would act as a vaporiser and kill the invaders. To-day the pad is soaked in nitro-benzine and this is quite successful in keeping bees free from acarine. The queen is always cherished and attended by her citizens, and is always one of the last to die when disease strikes.

Mr Crowson has one very unusual story to tell: 'Once I was called to a hotel that I used to visit; they had bees in the garden there, but they had a gardener who wouldn't have anything to do with them. So I was called in one winter's night: "Could I come? SOS!" It was a hotel right out in the open. "Would I come, as a lady visitor had been stung in the bath and the bees were coming into the bathroom!" That was queer, I thought, and in winter too. Anyway, I got some things together and I went over there. Well, what had happened, there was a room downstairs which had been turned into a bathroom and it had a chimney. The chimney had been covered over with a sheet of plywood and the lady had gone to have a bath and the vibration which the pipes made had disturbed the bees. But why were they down there? This was on the ground floor. So I scraped up the bees and when I did, I found out what had happened. Jackdaws like chimneys, or they certainly do round here; they drop sticks down until one lodges and then they build on top of that, you see, and before you know where you are, they are up near the top. The jackdaws bring their brood there each year, during the breeding season. What had happened was that in time, the sticks had rotted and down had come the lot. I gathered up all this rubbish with the bees, and tried to separate them. I put them in a cardboard box and I found there was a nest that had come down with the sticks with mummified jackdaws in it! Baby jackdaws had been killed and mummified with propolis from the bees.'

Propolis is a resinous substance gathered by bees from buds and used by them to stop up crevices. Fir trees are a favourite source, and the strong perfume of pine will confirm whether it has been collected from this tree.

'I brought the bees back home and didn't know what to do with them, so I tipped them out in front of a small hive already occupied by bees. Next morning, I found there had been a terrible slaughter.' Although it was in the dead of winter, Mr Crowson believes the new bees had killed the bees that were hibernating.

Mr Crowson used to exhibit his honey at a number of shows where honey was judged for its attraction, cleanliness, clearness and taste. 'Anything to make a bit of money,' he smiled. He thinks this probably earned him more than breeding. He once thought he would try to win the silver cup at Kew and decided to enter the open class, as he was not a member of the local association. He carefully packed up his honey to be transported by rail, but unfortunately it was never delivered to the show: it was left behind on the station. 'Sometimes things were the same then as they are now,' Mr Crowson remarked. However, not quite: the stationmaster sent his apologies! Undaunted, Mr Crowson entered the competition again the following year and, not surprisingly, he won the cup!

NOTE: Sadly, Mr H.W. Crowson passed away soon after our meeting in 1993.

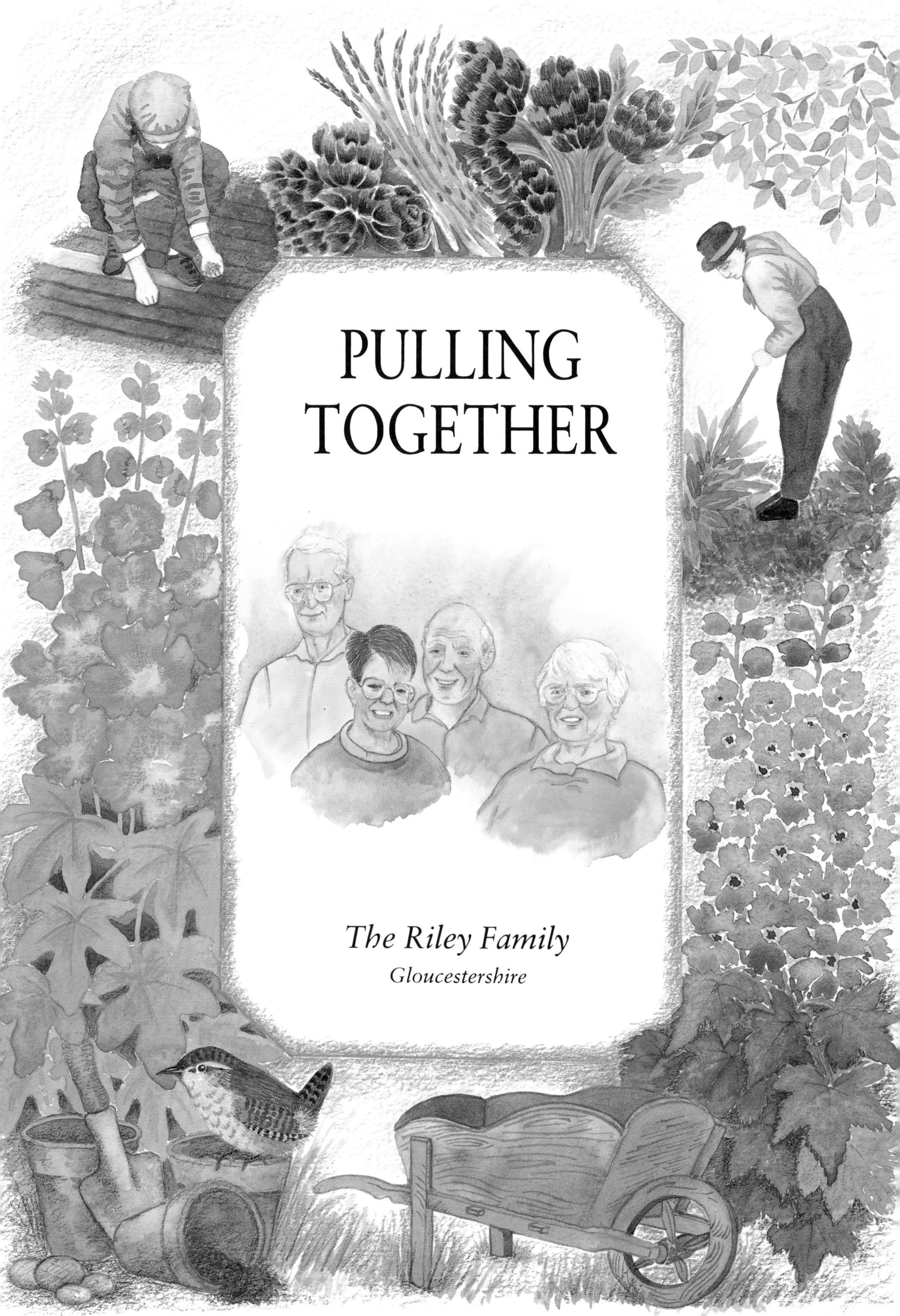
PULLING
TOGETHER
The Riley Family
Gloucestershire

Ralph and Edna Riley settled at The Scarr in 1959 when they were in their early thirties; Ralph had already worked in market gardening, and by that time they wanted a place of their own. Both Edna and Ralph were overjoyed when they were allocated a smallholding by the Land Settlement Association, agents for the Ministry of Agriculture and Fisheries which owned estates throughout England. This was an organisation that had been set up many years earlier to help resettle miners from Durham and Wales during the Depression. An interview had followed the Rileys answer to an advertisement in the *Evesham Gazette*; the next step was to get together the £500 capital they were expected to put into their new venture. This was matched by a substantial loan of £1,500 from the association, to enable them to equip the smallholding. Even so, they were still stretched financially.

They moved into the three-bedroom house and soon got to work on their three-acre plot, making use of the landlord's glasshouse, erected when the LSA first began the scheme. (On all holdings there was a heated glasshouse which usually measured 60 by 25 feet.) One of the Rileys' first priorities was to increase the glass: Ralph purchased timber and erected the framework, and when the glazed 'Dutch lights' arrived, neighbours rallied round to help him. There was a fine community spirit then; today they might have to pay for labour.

Ralph set to and prepared for lettuce to be planted under glass, and they cut their first crop in March. However, it seemed a long time until they were paid in mid-April. They decided to grow lettuce both inside and out, so a second crop was sown under glass to be raised indoors and planted outside as soon as the soil was warm enough to give a continuous crop. They also grew potatoes, strawberries, celery and radishes, and picked gooseberries from the bushes already there.

It was a big co-operative when they first arrived, and the estate did the packing, grading, marketing and selling. Under their tenancy agreement everything was sold through the packing shed run by the association, and this was the strength of the system: the manager knew the demands of the market, and after discussion with the tenants they agreed upon the varieties to be grown. All the supplies required were made available from the stores, Edna recalls. 'They could buy all the things they needed, like manures, seeds, peat, equipment and their tools – everything, and it would be open every day. It was a great place for the men to go up to and have a chat. And why not? It's quite a lonely job.'

A propagating service was provided too, where the plants (especially tomato

Tim Riley and his sister

plants) were propagated and supplied to the tenants. The estate manager was there to be consulted on problems, and the association kept all the tenants' accounts. It was felt these arrangements would relieve new tenants of the problems of management, would leave them free to devote their whole time to production, and help them settle down with less anxiety.

Eventually, in 1983, the Land Settlement Association ceased to operate, and the tenants were surprised to be given the opportunity to buy their properties. The announcement was made in parliament and was received with mixed feelings. Many were glad; they felt that although each estate owned by the association had a tenant's committee and a democratic process to air grievances, it was a top-heavy paternalistic organisation made distant because the head office was in London.

'Tenants had become vocal and self-confident and wanted to be more in command of their own affairs.' Under the packing shed arrangement they had no control over prices, and could only tell at the end of the year whether they had made a reasonable living or not. On the other hand, now they had to find their own market, so Ralph explained: 'It was all one big co-operative then, and all our bits and pieces put together made a good contribution, where we could have a certain strength in marketing to deal with the supermarkets and wholesalers.'

Ralph is a contented person, and he and his son work happily together. Had the LSA continued to operate there may have been the possibility of Tim getting his own tenancy; instead he is now building his own house, and is in partnership with his father. Tim is married to Marie José, a young Dutch landscape architect whose family has a shrub and tree nursery in Holland. Ralph wanted to keep Tim 'out of it, because it is a poorish living'; but even as a tiny boy Tim thought it was preferable 'to do real work at home' rather than go to school. However, Tim finally studied at Pershore College of Horticulture, and although he feels that his course was too broad to be particularly relevant to the specialised work he is doing now, he is glad of the opportunity it gave him to know his way round the industry.

The Rileys have now decided to specialise in one crop: they grow tomatoes under glass and have chosen the variety known as 'Liberto' as this has a firm skin and travels well. Everything on the smallholding is set up for tomato-growing, and it is all controlled by computer. Tim explains: 'You've got to have a bit of a "feel" for the crop, but it's more of a science now . . . Now you look up "Tomatoes" in the computer book and set your computer . . . The computer tells you what temperature to run it at; it will tell you exactly what nutrients are needed and what the ph must be.'

But Ralph misses the old days, going into the glasshouse and sniffing the atmosphere, and thinking the plants want some more water, or need more ventilation. 'There's no time for that, when each man has to have an output of two or three times what he did in the sixties, to make it all profitable' his son reminds him. 'It's all automatic now. In fact these days it's a bit more boring and can get fairly tedious.' Ralph misses the instinctive side, and there could be complications, as Edna points out:

'Last year they went off to a conference together and I knew only vaguely where it was to be held. I went up after lunch and the ventilator hadn't opened; it was like a Turkish bath up there, and there wasn't a thing I could do about it manually and I didn't know what buttons to press. I had to make about eight 'phone calls until eventually I got them, and Tim said, "Well, press this and this and this" – and they opened. It was a worry, you can't really do anything about it. In that huge glasshouse there is only that one door, and the amount of air circulation was nil!'

Tim is philosophical: 'The thing with technology is you have to insure.' However, they have an alarm bell in the house in case something goes wrong.

One essential thing today is for the market gardener to be a good welder, and this is one of the most useful skills that Tim learned at college . . . 'There is so much piping installed in the glasshouse, and it must all be well maintained. If that were put to an outside contractor it could be disastrous financially.'

The Rileys believe the more they can do for themselves and not rely on outside help, the better. However, they are aware of the false economy of inadequate DIY methods and have been successful in creating a happy marriage of old-fashioned 'make-do-and-mend' habits with new technology. Old pram wheels turned their ventilators in the old days: now they have a system of battery-propelled trolleys, manufactured by them on the premises, that are used for training the crop. Push trolleys, for collecting tomatoes, now run along rails between the rows of plants and the saving in time spent harvesting is very considerable.

The Rileys are proud of their system of burning sawdust to produce cheap heat for their glasshouses; it is more economical than oil, though a good supply of sawdust is needed and a large area of good, dry storage space. The latter is provided by a large plastic tunnel; they once had eight of these in use for cultivation purposes, but found them impractical against the wind. Three tons of sawdust a week are bought in from the local ladder and fencing industry. The expense is in handling. A trailer and a large enough tractor are needed to move the stuff about, and a large scoop so that the sawdust can be dumped into the hopper; an auger then feeds the sawdust into the incinerator. The furnace equipment is expensive, too. So, overall there is a two-or three-year payback, even though they use a great deal of secondhand equipment. If they had not set up their system a few years ago they would not be able to do so now; the capital required would be too high.

No soil is used in growing tomatoes; instead, blocks of Rockwool, a bi-product of basalt, are imported from Denmark to take its place. Together with the perfect

WILLIAM COOPER, Ltd., 761, Old Kent Road, London, S.E.

Materials required for Building Span Roof Cucumber House, 100ft. by 12ft., as illustration.

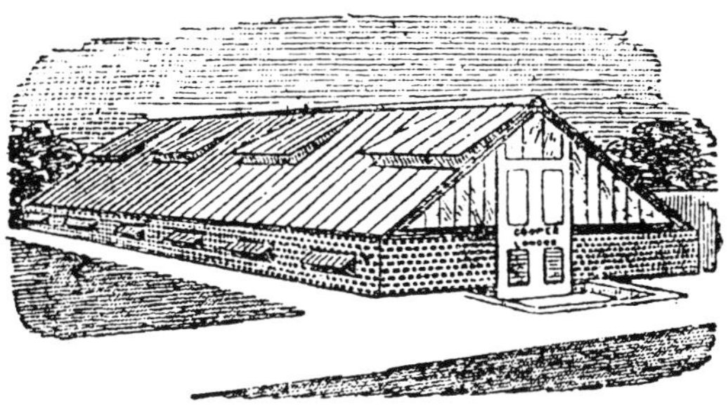

No. 555.

SPECIFICATION.

Good, sound, well-seasoned timbers, all planed, rabbeted, &c., ready for use. Ends, Door, and Ventilators made. Any handy man can erect.

Any alteration can be made to suit any size house at a corresponding alteration in price.

1 pair Ends (made), as illustration,
105ft. $1\frac{1}{4}$in. by 6in. Ridge,
105ft. 1in. by 4in. Capping,
230ft. 3in. by $3\frac{1}{2}$in. Plate,
210 $\frac{3}{4}$in. by 3in. Drip,
120—8ft. $1\frac{1}{4}$in. by 3in. Bars,
15 Ventilators, about 4ft. by 2ft.,
15 ditto Seats, about 60ft.,
1 Door, 6ft. by 2ft. 6in.

CAREFULLY PUT ON RAIL AT OUR WORKS FOR THE SUM OF £10.

When two or more Houses are required for building in one block Centre Gutters will be supplied at same price. Special quotation for Glass, Paint, and Heating Apparatus; also for erecting in any part free on application.

Cooper's Ready-mixed Paint.

No. 556.

The Most Reliable, Quick-drying, Ready-mixed Paint in the Trade.
Will stand any weather.
Made in all Colours. Tins Free.
Carriage Forward.
7lbs. 2s., 14lbs. 3s. 9d., 28lbs. 7s., 56lbs. 13s. 6d., 112lbs. 25s.
Packing, if desired, 3d. per 7lb. extra.
Try a Sample Tin. State colour required when ordering.
Prices quoted are subject to market fluctuations.

386

Edna and Ralph packing and hosing celery

balance of air, food and water and absence of disease, these blocks have proved more successful than soil. First, a seed is sown in a little block; when this has germinated and two leaves have appeared, it is then planted on; and finally, when it is about eight inches high, it is planted into a slab of Rockwool and the roots will grow through and anchor it. Plants are now producing as many as twenty-five trusses.

Harvesting is a busy time: Monday, Wednesday and Friday mornings are spent harvesting and packing; the afternoons and all day Tuesdays and Thursdays are spent tending the crop: 'Two of us start picking at 7.30 in the morning and hope to have picked and packed and be ready for market by midday. We pack about seventy tons in a season.'

At the end of the season the haulm is taken out and burnt, and the glasshouse is fumigated and left for three or four days. The slabs will be stacked up on a pallet and sterilised with steam, and can then be used again.

Until two or three years ago it was necessary to go round the glasshouse vibrating the plants with an electrical instrument to ensure pollination. Nowadays this process has been eliminated by the installation of 'bee boxes': these contain small colonies of

a fairly tolerant variety of bumble bee. The boxes are fixed to the wall of the glasshouse, and because the bees do not regenerate themselves the boxes are removed and replaced about every month. The bees work the flowers for their pollen, but there is no nectar. The interior of the boxes have cells that take syrup and on the side of the boxes there is a feeder for replenishing the supply.

In the glasshouse, whitefly is controlled biologically: the eggs of the encarsia wasp are secured to a card and these are hung on plants around the greenhouses; when the adults hatch out they parasiticide the whitefly. 'This has proved to be cheaper than any other method of control.'

There have been some problems with marketing. Once, proficient growers set out to beat the market and get their produce to the shops first; 'Now there is no market to beat.' Improved transport and storage facilities have allowed supplies to come in from distant lands to be available all year round. Nevertheless, the Rileys are optimistic. They are all set up for tomato growing, so for them at present there are no alternatives; but they know they are doing a good job and look forward to the future. Modern technology has made things easier for them, and now it is possible for them to take holidays!

"HOPE YOU COME
WHEN MY
GARDEN'S NICE!"

ACKNOWLEDGEMENTS

We would like to thank all those gardeners who have shared the stories of their lives with us. Without their help this book could not have been written.

Our thanks also go to Jean Painter, matron at Red Oaks, The Gardeners' Country Home, Henfield; and Mrs M. Deacon, affectionately known by the residents at nearby Rayner Court as 'Bubbles'.

We also extend thanks to the staff of the Royal Horticultural Society Library, the National Trust, and of Westonbirt School. The help of Deborah Risby and Helen Davies of Cadbury's Bournville, and Jean Savage of Hillier Nurseries, Ampfield, has been very much appreciated. Many thanks to Sue Hall of David & Charles for her support and help, and to Avis Murray for her illustrations. Thanks also to Philip Murphy for illustrating the jacket.

The quotation from 'The Women's Land Army' has been reproduced by permission of Curtis Brown, London, on behalf of the Estate of Vita Sackville-West.

Photographs of Dennis Lindup appearing on pages 109 and 118 are reproduced by kind permission of the *Birmingham Post & Mail* Limited.

INDEX

Page references in *italics* refer to illustrations